Do The Maths

How to Calculate Whether You Should Lease or Buy

Colin Tourick

Eyelevel Books

Do The Maths
Colin Tourick

© Colin Tourick 2013

Published by:

Eyelevel Books
Worcester

www.eyelevelbooks.co.uk

Printed and bound by CPI Group (UK) Ltd, Croydon, CR0 4YY

Cover 'numbers' image courtesy of Fleet World.

ISBN 978 1902528 35 9

Do The Maths

How to Calculate Whether
You Should Lease or Buy

Colin Tourick

FOREWORD

People write books for all sorts of reasons. Some have a burning desire to tell a story whilst others feel they have a book 'inside them' that they just have to get published.

My own motivation for writing this book is much simpler: I wish someone had given me something like this when I first started my career in asset finance! I had worked in the industry for some considerable time before I had finally pieced together an understanding of the mathematics of asset finance, the various funding products that were available and how tax affected lease v buy calculations.

This book is designed to be a primer in asset finance. It will walk you through the basic principles and help you to do your own calculations using some of the great tools available in Excel.

In time I may produce a second edition of this book. If you have any thoughts on how the book could be improved, please contact me via www.tourick.com

I need to thank a number of people who have contributed to the production of the book.

First, a big thank you Volkswagen Financial Services, Fleet Operations Limited, Jaama Limited and Visper Asset Finance Limited. Their sponsorship has made this book possible and I am proud that the front cover sports their logos.

Next, thank you to Fleet World. They asked me to write a monthly column and were kind enough to allow me to choose my own topic, so I chose the mathematics of leasing. Those columns have formed the core material of this book.

And last but not least, thank you to Jon Moore the publisher at Eyelevel Books. This is the tenth book of mine that they have published and once again Jon has done a sterling job.

Professor Colin Tourick
London
January 2013

CONTENTS

INTRODUCTION

This book is a primer in asset finance and leasing. It offers a step-by-step guide to the mathematics of asset finance and explains the features of each of the various products you are likely to come across in the asset finance market.

Your business may be based in the UK, USA, somewhere in Europe or indeed any country in the world. You may be thinking about buying a machine tool, printing press, computer system, fleet of buses or a company car. And you may be reading this book soon after the publication date in 2013 or several years later.

This book sets out to explain the underlying principles which you can apply in any country, for any kind of asset and under any set of tax rules.

To provide examples for every country, asset type or tax regime would be impossible, especially as tax rules change every year.

Therefore we will focus on the financing of one type of asset (company cars) in one country (the United Kingdom) using the tax rules that were in place when this material was originally published in Fleet World between 2010 and 2012.

Once we get to the subject of taxation I will explain the rules that applied to the financing of cars in the UK in that period and you will be able to see how those rules affect the cash flows.

To make the examples work in your country and your tax regime, for the class of assets you are interested in financing, all you need to do is to work out how your tax rules differ from the rules in the examples and change the cash flows accordingly.

1

SHOULD YOU LEASE OR BUY YOUR VEHICLES?

IN THIS CHAPTER...

- Discounted cash flow analysis (DCF)

- Simple DCF examples

- Present value

- Time value of money

Many businesses lease their vehicles and are very happy with the arrangement. Many others buy their vehicles and are equally happy with that arrangement.

Ask both groups why they prefer their option and they will give you a long list to justify their decision.

Those in the buying camp may talk about flexibility, control, no early termination or extension charges, the benefit of capital allowances, and so on. Those in the leasing camp may talk about simplicity, discounts, cost and risk management, and so on.

This book addresses this question – should you lease or buy your vehicles? – from a completely different perspective: a scientific perspective. It seeks to find the answer to the question, "How can I calculate whether I should buy or lease my vehicles?"

The key word is 'calculate'. This book is all about finance and mathematics. In order to decide whether to lease or buy your vehicles you will need to carry out a financial evaluation. This book shows you how.

Let's take a simple example. You are about to buy a new car for £10,000 and expect to sell it in three years for £3,000. You normally borrow from the bank. Let's say the bank currently charges you 10% p.a. However the car salesman suggests that instead of buying the car you enter a non-maintenance contract hire agreement (a lease). The rentals will be £2,800 payable annually in advance.

You need to decide whether to lease or buy.

You might be thinking; "Why change? I've always used bank loans. I bet he earns more commission on contract hire. Is it better to pay three rentals of £2,800 or to pay £10,000 now, pay the loan interest then get back £3,000 in three years' time?"

You need a tool to be able to make these comparisons and the best tool that we have is *discounted cash flow analysis* (DCF).

DCF uses the idea of the *time value of money*. £1 received in a year's time is worth less than £1 received today, because you could invest £1 today to generate more over the year and also because inflation will reduce the value of that £1 over the year.

It uses interest rates to 'discount' (i.e., to reduce) future cash flows to 'today's' value (present value, or PV). Then the PVs of all of the cash flows of each option – lease or buy – are added up and the option with the highest PV (or the lowest negative PV) is the winner.

So, let's evaluate the options:

1   YOU COULD BUY THE VEHICLE AND SELL IT IN THREE YEARS

£10,000 paid today is, obviously, £10,000 in today's money (PV).

Next you need to determine the PV of the £3,000 receivable in three years. We do this by discounting (reducing) the £3,000 by an interest rate, 10% per annum, using compound interest.

A simple way to think of this is to ask 'How much would I have to invest today to give me £3,000 in three years if I were to earn 10% per annum interest? The answer is £2,253.94, and this spreadsheet proves that this figure is correct.

Year	Start balance £	Interest at 10% p.a. £	End balance £
1	2,253.94	225.39	2,479.34
2	2,479.34	247.93	2,727.27
3	2,727.27	272.73	3,000.00

You could calculate this using trial and error or using Excel's 'goal seek' function.

An easier way to do it is to use a calculator to work out the value of the formula: $1 \div (1.1)^3$.

That is, one divided by 1.1 raised to the power of 3.

The steps here are as follows:

■ Work out 1.1 to the power of 3. i.e. 1.1 x 1.1 x 1.1 = 1.331.

■ Then divide 1.331 into 1, i.e. 1 ÷ 1.331.

■ The answer is 0.751315. This is called the *discount factor*.

■ Then multiply the discount factor by £3,000.

The answer is £2,253.94 (£2,253.944 before rounding)

This is the PV of £3,000 received in three years' time when the discount rate is 10% per annum.

The reason you needed to work first with 1.1 is that 0.1 is 10% and for the DCF arithmetic to work you have to place the 10% after the number 1. So if, for example, you wanted to work out the discount factor for 8% over 4 years, you would use $1 \div (1.08)^4$.

Going back to the original example; if you buy the car now you will pay out £10,000 and receive £2,253.94 in 'today's money', so the net cost to you today is £7,746.06.

(This is the net cost to you but not necessarily to someone else. If their borrowing rate is 12% they will arrive at a different answer.)

2 ALTERNATIVELY, YOU COULD LEASE THE VEHICLE FOR THREE YEARS

Each rental falls due at a different time so you now have to do three discounting calculations; after one, two and three years. You will need different discount factors for each of these payments to discount the value of the rental to PV terms.

We saw that solving $1 \div (1.1)^3$ gave us the discount factor for a cash flow arising in three years' time. Similarly, $1 \div (1.1)^2$ is the discount factor for a cash flow arising in two years' time, which is the date the last rental would be payable under the lease.

$1 \div (1.1)^1$, that is, $1 \div 1.1$, is the discount factor for the first rental and $1 \div (1.1)^0$ is the discount factor for any payment on day one. However, $1 \div (1.1)^0 = 1$, reflecting the fact that there is no need to discount a cash flow that occurs on day one.

We then add up the present values of the three discounted rentals and see that they total £7,659.50, as shown opposite.

The chart shows how we can then compare the two options.

Option 1: PURCHASE			
Buy for £10,000 today and receive £3,000 in three years			
Determine value of £3,000 in three years at today's value (present value)			
The discount rate is	$1 \div (1.1)^3 = 0.751315$		
So	£3,000	x 0.751315 =	£ 2,253.94
Less: Outlay today			£10,000.00
Present value			-£ 7,746.06
Option 2: LEASE			
Pay £2,800 p.a. starting today, for three years			
1st rental (This occurs today so there is no need to discount it)			-£2,800.00
2nd rental	£2,800 ÷ 1.1	0.909091 =	-£2,545.45
3rd rental	$£2,800 \div (1.1)^2$	0.826446 =	-£2,314.05
			-£7,659.50
So leasing is cheaper than buying by			**£86.55**

So now we have our two options:

■ Buy for a PV of £7,746.06 or

■ Lease for a PV of £7,659.50

If you lease you will save £86.55 in present value terms.

If there are no other factors that you need to consider, this proves you should opt for the lease and save £86.55.

This has been a very simple example. Normally payments would be more frequent and you'd include the tax effects. We will look at more complex examples later.

You can use discounted cash flow to select between contract hire, contract purchase, hire purchase, lease purchase, salary sacrifice and outright purchase decisions, in fact any time you have to choose between alternatives that involve different cash flows.

2

USING DISCOUNT FACTORS TO FIND OUT WHETHER YOU SHOULD LEASE OR BUY

IN THIS CHAPTER...

■ Calculating with monthly discount factors

■ Using Excel for simple evaluations

■ The standard discounting formula

■ Adding up discounted amounts

In chapter 1 we looked at the type of financial evaluation you need to carry out when deciding whether to lease or buy your vehicles (or any other asset for that matter). The example was very simple (for example it used annual rather than monthly cash flows) but it did allow us to introduce some key concepts:

1 Money has a 'time value'. You'd prefer to receive £1 today rather than £1 in a year's time.

2 Discounted cash flow analysis. We can use interest rates to 'discount' future cash flows to 'today's' values (present value, or PV), so that every cash flow can then be viewed as if it had arisen today. This allows us to add up the PVs of all of the cash flows of each option, and the option with the highest PV (or the lowest negative PV) is the winner.

We are now going to produce a lease v buy evaluation using monthly discount factors.

As ever with DCF there are several ways we could do this. For example, we could use a financial calculator or just run through the algebra. However, in this instance we will use Excel, because Excel can be found on almost everyone's PC and it provides a very visible result.

The first step is to calculate the monthly 'discount factors' we will need.

As we saw in chapter 1, a discount factor is the amount by which you need to multiply a future cash flow in order to discount (i.e. reduce) it to today's (present) value.

Let's assume you have the choice between:

■ leasing a car for 3 years at £259.90 per month, or

■ buying it for £10,000 on overdraft today and then selling it for an estimated £2,900 in 36 months.

Which would you prefer? At first glance it's not easy to see which is going to be cheaper.

Would it help if we knew that your overdraft rate is 1% per month? Possibly, though it's still hard to do the calculations using mental arithmetic. We need to do a Lease v Buy analysis to work out the cheapest option.

To do this, you first need to set up an Excel spreadsheet with the headings shown in cells C1 to F2 opposite. Next, enter the month numbers, 1-37. Then enter the 1% monthly overdraft rate into cell A1. It needs to be the monthly rate rather than the annual rate and this needs to be shown as 0.01 (because to calculate 1% of a number you multiply it by 0.01).

Now for the juicy bit: calculating the discount factors.

Month 1 is easy. As the first rental or the purchase price would be paid on day 1, i.e. 'today', there's no need to discount these, they're already at Present Value.

Month 2 (the figure in B5) is calculated by using the standard discounting formula:

$$\frac{1}{(1+i)^n}$$

In Excel-speak this translates into 1/(1+$A$1)^1.

$A$1 is Excel's way of saying 'always use the number in cell A1'

What this is saying for month 2 is:

"One, divided by ((one plus the monthly interest rate) raised to the power of 1), equals 0.99009901."

In other words, just over 99%. It is conventional to calculate discount factors as a decimal value rather than a percentage.

If you had the option of paying £259.90 today or £257.33 in a month, and your normal money cost was 1% per month, you'd be just as happy paying either amount because £257.33 x 1.01 = £259.90.

	A	B	C	D	E	F
			Lease		Buy	
1	0.01		Cash flow	PV	Cash flow	PV
2						
3	Month	Discount factors				
4	1	1.00000000	-£259.90	-£259.90	-£10,000.00	-£10,000.00
5	2	0.99009901	-£259.90	-£257.33		
6	3	0.98029605	-£259.90	-£254.78		
7	4	0.97059015	-£259.90	-£252.26		
8	5	0.96098034	-£259.90	-£249.76		
9	6	0.95146569	-£259.90	-£247.29		
10	7	0.94204524	-£259.90	-£244.84		
11	8	0.93271805	-£259.90	-£242.41		
12	9	0.92348322	-£259.90	-£240.01		
13	10	0.91433982	-£259.90	-£237.64		
14	11	0.90528695	-£259.90	-£235.28		
15	12	0.89632372	-£259.90	-£232.95		
16	13	0.88744923	-£259.90	-£230.65		
17	14	0.87866260	-£259.90	-£228.36		
18	15	0.86996297	-£259.90	-£226.10		
19	16	0.86134947	-£259.90	-£223.86		
20	17	0.85282126	-£259.90	-£221.65		
21	18	0.84437749	-£259.90	-£219.45		
22	19	0.83601731	-£259.90	-£217.28		
23	20	0.82773992	-£259.90	-£215.13		
24	21	0.81954447	-£259.90	-£213.00		
25	22	0.81143017	-£259.90	-£210.89		
26	23	0.80339621	-£259.90	-£208.80		
27	24	0.79544179	-£259.90	-£206.74		
28	25	0.78756613	-£259.90	-£204.69		
29	26	0.77976844	-£259.90	-£202.66		
30	27	0.77204796	-£259.90	-£200.66		
31	28	0.76440392	-£259.90	-£198.67		
32	29	0.75683557	-£259.90	-£196.70		
33	30	0.74934215	-£259.90	-£194.75		
34	31	0.74192292	-£259.90	-£192.83		
35	32	0.73457715	-£259.90	-£190.92		
36	33	0.72730411	-£259.90	-£189.03		
37	34	0.72010307	-£259.90	-£187.15		
38	35	0.71297334	-£259.90	-£185.30		
39	36	0.70591420	-£259.90	-£183.47		
40	37	0.69892495			£2,900.00	£2,026.88
41				-£7,903.19		-£7,973.12
42	Difference					-£69.93

To calculate the discount rates for all subsequent months, you just have to raise the result by one extra power in each month; i.e.

■ month 3 (the figure in B6) is calculated using the formula =1/(1+$A$1)^2

■ month 4 (the figure in B7) is calculated using the formula =1/(1+$A$1)^3

■ And so on up to month 37 which is calculated using the formula =1/(1+$A$1)^36.

We've continued to month 37 because the last lease rental would be paid at the beginning of month 36 but the sale proceeds for the car, if outright purchased, would arrive at the end of that month. Hence we need to include the extra month.

The result of this work is that we now have a stream of discount factors running from month 1–37. These factors are for a 1% per month interest rate. If you wish you can easily change the interest rate by altering the figure in cell A1 and this would give you a new set of discount factors.

Now that we've calculated the discount factors, we can start using them. In columns C and E, type in the actual cash flows that are going to occur under the two options, lease and buy. Be careful with the signs; a minus shows you are paying something out, a plus shows you are receiving it.

Next, in columns D and F, multiply the contents of C and E, respectively, by the discount factors in column B.

Then add up columns D and F, and work out the difference.

You have now produced a series of discount factors and used these to discount the cash flows of the two options. By using interest rates you have 'discounted' (i.e. reduced) the value of future cash flows to today's values and this has allowed you to add them up and compare them as if they were all occurring today.

So, you now have your two options:

- Buy for a PV of £7,973.12 or
- Lease for a PV of £7,903.19

So leasing will save you £69.93.

3

LEASING MATHS USING EXCEL

In chapter 2 we looked at how to calculate Discounted Cash Flow discount factors. In this chapter we will look at:

- how to calculate the monthly finance instalment (or the rental) when you know the interest rate, and

- how to calculate the interest rate when you know the monthly instalment.

Let's assume we are looking at a simple lease purchase agreement on a £15,000 car.

A lease purchase agreement is a hire purchase (or conditional sale) agreement with a balloon payment at the end of the agreement. We discuss different types of agreement in a later chapter.

Let's assume that under this agreement you are being asked to pay £345.27 per month on a 3+21 payment pattern, followed by two months in which you pay nothing, and you then have to pay an £8,000 balloon payment at the end of the agreement.

The first chart (on the next page) shows you the result we want to get to.

You'll see that we have a 24 month agreement. On day 1 you pay 3 times the normal monthly instalment, which means you then 'owe' the funder £13,964.19 for the month.

Interest of £69.82 (at 6% p.a.) has accrued by the end of the month, so as you go into the new month the balance outstanding is £14,034.01.

You then make the first regular monthly payment of £345.27, interest accrues for month 2 and from then on this same pattern continues until the end of month 22.

At the start of months 23 and 24 you pay nothing, so in those months you simply accrue interest at the end of the month.

	A	B	C	D	E	F
1	Month	Opening balance	Payment	sub-total	Interest	Closing balance
2	1	£15,000.00	£1,035.81	£13,964.19	£69.82	£14,034.01
3	2	£14,034.01	£345.27	£13,688.74	£68.44	£13,757.19
4	3	£13,757.19	£345.27	£13,411.92	£67.06	£13,478.98
5	4	£13,478.98	£345.27	£13,133.71	£65.67	£13,199.38
6	5	£13,199.38	£345.27	£12,854.11	£64.27	£12,918.38
7	6	£12,918.38	£345.27	£12,573.11	£62.87	£12,635.98
8	7	£12,635.98	£345.27	£12,290.71	£61.45	£12,352.16
9	8	£12,352.16	£345.27	£12,006.89	£60.03	£12,066.92
10	9	£12,066.92	£345.27	£11,721.66	£58.61	£11,780.26
11	10	£11,780.26	£345.27	£11,434.99	£57.17	£11,492.17
12	11	£11,492.17	£345.27	£11,146.90	£55.73	£11,202.63
13	12	£11,202.63	£345.27	£10,857.37	£54.29	£10,911.65
14	13	£10,911.65	£345.27	£10,566.38	£52.83	£10,619.22
15	14	£10,619.22	£345.27	£10,273.95	£51.37	£10,325.32
16	15	£10,325.32	£345.27	£9,980.05	£49.90	£10,029.95
17	16	£10,029.95	£345.27	£9,684.68	£48.42	£9,733.10
18	17	£9,733.10	£345.27	£9,387.83	£46.94	£9,434.77
19	18	£9,434.77	£345.27	£9,089.50	£45.45	£9,134.95
20	19	£9,134.95	£345.27	£8,789.68	£43.95	£8,833.63
21	20	£8,833.63	£345.27	£8,488.36	£42.44	£8,530.80
22	21	£8,530.80	£345.27	£8,185.53	£40.93	£8,226.46
23	22	£8,226.46	£345.27	£7,881.19	£39.41	£7,920.60
24	23	£7,920.60	£0.00	£7,920.60	£39.60	£7,960.20
25	24	£7,960.20	£0.00	£7,960.20	£39.80	£8,000.00
26						
27	Payment		Interest			
28	£345.27		6.0%			

Therefore, by the end of month 24 you owe £8,000 which you pay as a balloon payment and the agreement then ends.

So, how do we build such a spreadsheet?

Here are the formulae you need to build into your spreadsheet. It's not as big a chore as it might seem. You just key in the formulae for the first two months and you can then highlight cells A3 to F3 and drag them down to row 25. By doing this you will have replicated month 2's formulae right down to month 24. The $ signs in the formulae in columns C and E will ensure you pick up the payments and interest from row 28.

	A	B	C	D	E	F
1	Month	Opening balance	Payment	sub-total	Interest	Closing balance
2	1	15000	=3*A28	=+B2-C2	=+D2*C$28/12	=+D2+E2
3	=+A2+1	=+F2	=+A$28	=+B3-C3	=+D3*C$28/12	=+D3+E3
4	=+A3+1	=+F3	=+A$28	=+B4-C4	=+D4*C$28/12	=+D4+E4
5	=+A4+1	=+F4	=+A$28	=+B5-C5	=+D5*C$28/12	=+D5+E5
6	=+A5+1	=+F5	=+A$28	=+B6-C6	=+D6*C$28/12	=+D6+E6
7	=+A6+1	=+F6	=+A$28	=+B7-C7	=+D7*C$28/12	=+D7+E7
8	=+A7+1	=+F7	=+A$28	=+B8-C8	=+D8*C$28/12	=+D8+E8
9	=+A8+1	=+F8	=+A$28	=+B9-C9	=+D9*C$28/12	=+D9+E9
10	=+A9+1	=+F9	=+A$28	=+B10-C10	=+D10*C$28/12	=+D10+E10
11	=+A10+1	=+F10	=+A$28	=+B11-C11	=+D11*C$28/12	=+D11+E11
12	=+A11+1	=+F11	=+A$28	=+B12-C12	=+D12*C$28/12	=+D12+E12
13	=+A12+1	=+F12	=+A$28	=+B13-C13	=+D13*C$28/12	=+D13+E13
14	=+A13+1	=+F13	=+A$28	=+B14-C14	=+D14*C$28/12	=+D14+E14
15	=+A14+1	=+F14	=+A$28	=+B15-C15	=+D15*C$28/12	=+D15+E15
16	=+A15+1	=+F15	=+A$28	=+B16-C16	=+D16*C$28/12	=+D16+E16
17	=+A16+1	=+F16	=+A$28	=+B17-C17	=+D17*C$28/12	=+D17+E17
18	=+A17+1	=+F17	=+A$28	=+B18-C18	=+D18*C$28/12	=+D18+E18
19	=+A18+1	=+F18	=+A$28	=+B19-C19	=+D19*C$28/12	=+D19+E19
20	=+A19+1	=+F19	=+A$28	=+B20-C20	=+D20*C$28/12	=+D20+E20
21	=+A20+1	=+F20	=+A$28	=+B21-C21	=+D21*C$28/12	=+D21+E21
22	=+A21+1	=+F21	=+A$28	=+B22-C22	=+D22*C$28/12	=+D22+E22
23	=+A22+1	=+F22	=+A$28	=+B23-C23	=+D23*C$28/12	=+D23+E23
24	=+A23+1	=+F23	0	=+B24-C24	=+D24*C$28/12	=+D24+E24
25	=+A24+1	=+F24	0	=+B25-C25	=+D25*C$28/12	=+D25+E25
26						
27	Payment		Interest			
28	345.269215880052		0.06			

- Column A simply generates the month number.

- Column B shows the amount outstanding at the start of each month; initially £15,000.

- Column C shows the payments you will make. Note the reference to A$28, which contains the monthly payment.

- Column D is a sub-total, which we need in order to calculate interest on the balance outstanding each month.

- Column E is the interest for the month, 6% p.a. (per C28). Note that 0.06 is the same as 6%, and that we take one twelfth for each month's interest.

- Column F is just the balance outstanding at the end of the month.

Remember what we are trying to do: produce a spreadsheet that allows us to calculate either the monthly payment or the interest rate. The magic feature of Excel that allows us to do this is called Goal Seek, which can be found in data > what-if analysis > goal seek in Excel 2007.

Once you've set up your spreadsheet you can start doing some interesting calculations. The spreadsheet currently shows that if the interest rate is 6% the payment is £345.27. Want to know how much the payment will be if the interest rate is 9% p.a?

Just change cell C28 to 0.09 (i.e., 9%). You'll see you've thrown the spreadsheet out of kilter because the final payment in cell F25 has increased from £8,000 to £8,708.47, which is clearly wrong. We need to change the monthly payment so that this amount returns to £8,000.

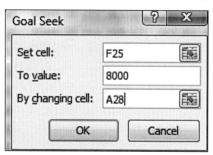

In order to do this, open up Goal Seek and tell it to Set Cell F25 to £8,000 by changing cell A28, then press OK.

Hey presto, the monthly payment in A28 (and everywhere else in the spreadsheet) changes to £371.75.

Like to know what the interest rate would be if the payment was £400? Change the monthly payment in A28 to £400, note that it's thrown the final payment out of kilter, then open up Goal Seek and tell it to Set Cell F25 back to £8,000 by changing the interest cell, C28. And the result is 12.2%.

You can now tinker with this basic spreadsheet to your heart's content, changing the payment pattern, contract length, payment profile, etc., so long as you use Goal Seek to make sure you always end up with the final payment you expect.

You find this a bit long-winded? I suppose you're right. You could easily use a financial calculator for these calculations or Excel's 'fx' functions. However, I always prefer to produce a detailed Excel spreadsheet. The trouble with a financial calculator or Excel's fx functions is that with those you can press a button, get an answer, and not be quite sure where it's come from or whether you've made a mistake. But if you build up your calculations step-by-step in an Excel spreadsheet you can see what's happening, every step of the way.

Although this example has been for a lease purchase agreement its basic structure can be used for most financial agreements, e.g. hire purchase, conditional sale, finance lease etc.

Things are slightly different with contract hire because there is no obligation to pay a balloon payment: the lessor builds a residual value into their evaluation instead and you normally wouldn't know how much this is. However, these spreadsheets show precisely the sort of logic your lessor would be using when calculating your rental.

Don't want to go to the trouble of producing these spreadsheets yourself?

You can download all of the spreadsheets in this book at www.tourick.com

4

INTEREST RATES

In chapter 3 we used Excel to calculate a monthly rental when you know the interest rate, and vice versa.

Now we will look at the various types of interest rate.

SIMPLE INTEREST

Someone agrees to lend you £100 if you pay them back £110 in 1 year.

You think "10% interest is payable in one year, so the interest rate is 10% p.a."

Now imagine instead that you borrow £100 and agree to repay £110 in one lump sum in six months' time. The lender says this is 10% interest.

"But surely", you say, "if it was 10% I should repay £105 not £110?"

"Ah yes", the lender says, "but that assumes I'm charging you 10% p.a. interest, whereas in fact I am just charging 10% interest."

This is simple interest. It ignores the period over which the money is borrowed or the frequency with which payments are made. It can easily cause confusion.

FLAT RATE

This is a different type of interest, which is calculated by:

- taking the total interest payable
- dividing this by the number of years of the loan
- dividing the result by the amount advanced and
- multiplying by 100.

If you borrowed £100 repayable in 36 equal monthly repayments of £3.61, with a total repayment of £130, you would calculate the flat rate as follows (ignoring a 4p rounding error):

- £130 – £100 = £30, the total amount of interest payable.

- £30 ÷ 3 = £10, the total interest divided by the number of years.

- £10 ÷ £100 x 100 = 10% p.a. flat.

This is a slightly more sophisticated approach than simple interest because it takes into account the period over which the money is borrowed.

But don't you feel uncomfortable that this interest rate ignored the fact you are making monthly payments? The interest rate here would be 10% p.a. even if you made all of the repayments in three years' time.

So flat rates are not particularly helpful either. They can deceive the unwary.

The *Consumer Credit Act* makes it illegal for consumers to be quoted simple or flat rates, so clearly Parliament agreed that these methods were unsatisfactory.

COMPOUND INTEREST

This method takes into account the amount and timing of your repayments and acknowledges that every loan repayment reduces the amount you owe the lender. It's a fairer approach, allowing you to compare interest rates across lenders and across different payment profiles (monthly, quarterly, in advance or arrears, with or without a balloon payment, etc.).

Sadly, you cannot calculate compound interest rates using mental arithmetic.

We now need to consider three different types of compound interest:

- nominal rates
- true rates and
- annual percentage rates (APRs).

NOMINAL RATE OF INTEREST

Mortgages and business loans are expressed in nominal rates.

Here you take the annual interest rate, based on the amount of interest to be paid in the year, and divide it by 12 to reflect monthly payments.

If you borrow £100 repayable in 12 equal repayments of £8.88 over twelve months, with a total repayment of £106.62 (less a 4p rounding difference), the nominal rate will be 1% per month. And 1% per month multiplied by 12 is 12% p.a.

This chart on the next page shows the loan being repaid.

The chart is quite straightforward. You can see how 1% per month is being charged and how £8.88 per month repays this loan in full.

The lender tells you this is 12% p.a. and this seems reasonable, as 1% per month multiplied by 12 is definitely 12%.

Or is it?

Well, actually it isn't but we need now to consider true rates of interest to demonstrate this.

Period	Balance at start of period	Interest at 1% per month	Repayment	Balance at end of period
	£	£	£	£
1	100.00	1.00	8.88	92.12
2	92.12	0.92	8.88	84.15
3	84.15	0.84	8.88	76.11
4	76.11	0.76	8.88	67.98
5	67.98	0.68	8.88	59.78
6	59.78	0.60	8.88	51.49
7	51.49	0.51	8.88	43.12
8	43.12	0.43	8.88	34.67
9	34.67	0.35	8.88	26.13
10	26.13	0.26	8.88	17.51
11	17.51	0.18	8.88	8.80
12	8.80	0.09	8.88	0.00
	Total	6.62	106.62	

TRUE RATE OF INTEREST

A true (or 'effective') rate takes into account the timing and amount of every cash flow that occurs during the life of the agreement. It takes the monthly interest rate and compounds this to arrive at the annual rate.

So 1% per month would be 12.68% p.a., calculated as follows:

1% = 0.01

Add 1 to this and it becomes 1.01

Raise this by the power of 12, that is, compound it twelve times and you get 1.01^{12}

$1.01^{12} = 1.1268$

$1.1268 - 1 = 0.1268$

$0.1268 \times 100 = 12.68\%$

So somehow 1% per month becomes 12.68% p.a. Can this be correct?

Yes, it is, as the simple example below shows. Let's say you borrow £100 and are charged 1% per month interest.

We saw above that 1% per month equals 12% p.a. nominal. If that's the case for a loan repaid monthly it must also be the case for a loan where interest is charged monthly and the whole debt is repaid at the end of the year. Let's assume the loan stays in place for 12 months and is then repaid in full. That must mean you should repay £112.00 at the end of the year, right? Let's see.

Month	Start	Interest @ 1% per month	End
	£	£	£
1	100.00	1.00	101.00
2	101.00	1.01	102.01
3	102.01	1.02	103.03
4	103.03	1.03	104.06
5	104.06	1.04	105.10
6	105.10	1.05	106.15
7	106.15	1.06	107.21
8	107.21	1.07	108.29
9	108.29	1.08	109.37
10	109.37	1.09	110.46
11	110.46	1.10	111.57
12	111.57	1.12	112.68

What happened here? 1% per month has not created a debt of £112.00 at the end of the year but £112.68. Why?

This is because the 1% interest charged every month was itself accruing interest in subsequent months. As that interest on interest grew, it cost you an extra £0.68.

So 1% per month is not the same as 12% p.a., it is actually 1% p.a. compounded 12 times, or 12.68% p.a.

Doesn't a nominal rate of 12% begin to look rather pointless now? It gives you no real idea of the true interest cost you will incur.

Flat rates can easily cause confusion. Nominal rates are better, but only tell half the story and always show a smaller figure than the true interest rate.

A borrower quoted 6.62% interest with monthly repayments will think it compares favourably to a 4.5% bank overdraft rate.

However, if the 6.62% is a flat rate it represents a 12.0% nominal rate, far higher than the 4.5% bank overdraft rate. And it represents a 12.68% true rate.

Many believe flat rates should be made illegal and only true rates should be quoted.

ANNUAL PERCENTAGE RATE (APR)

While we might debate the 'best' interest rate to use in business-to-business transactions, flat and nominal rates have already been banned in consumer lending. The *Consumer Credit Act* says the annual percentage rate (APR) is the only acceptable rate. The APR is the true rate of interest (rounded to the nearest decimal point) taking into account any fees or other amounts payable to the lender.

We saw above that 1% per month gives a true rate of 12.68% p.a. If you simply had to repay £112.68 at the end of the year, the APR would be 12.68% rounded to the nearest one decimal point, i.e. 12.7%.

Imagine now that the lender also charges a £10 up-front arrangement fee. This makes the total amount payable £122.68, so the total charge for credit is £22.68. This is 22.68% of the amount borrowed. Rounded to the nearest decimal point, this becomes 22.7% APR.

5

USING EXCEL TO MAKE LEASE v BUY DECISIONS

IN THIS CHAPTER...

- More complex DCF calculations

- Building a more complex spreadsheet, step by step

- Using Excel to select between different financing options

- Proof that leasing maths can be fun

In this chapter we will take a look at a more complex form of DCF calculation.

We have already seen just how valuable a tool DCF can be. It's fundamental if you want to compare a number of financial proposals and decide which works best for you.

Which is better for you; outright purchase, hire purchase, lease purchase, finance lease, contract hire, contract purchase, employee car ownership scheme or salary sacrifice? DCF can give you the answer.

We've already looked at:

■ how to use Excel to calculate the monthly finance instalment (or rental) on a finance deal when you know the interest rate, and

■ how to calculate the interest rate when you know the monthly payment.

So in this chapter we are going to use Excel to do a complex DCF calculation.

Let's say you are about to add a car to your fleet and you are deciding how to finance it. You don't have any spare cash, so all of your payments will come out of your overdraft (on which you currently pay interest at 5.5% p.a. nominal).

Let's assume you have two options:

■ lease the car on a non-maintenance contract hire agreement for £400 per month on a 3+21 basis (i.e. you pay 3 months' rentals on day 1 and nothing at the start of months 23 and 24), or

■ buy it on lease purchase for a deposit of £2,400 followed by 23 equal monthly payments of £340 and a balloon payment of £7,500. You particularly like this option because the monthly payments are so low. You reckon the car will be worth around £8,000 after 2 years and that you'll probably sell it immediately.

How should you decide between these options?

This is where Excel can come to the rescue. It can discount (reduce) all of the cash flows to today's value (present value) and give you one number – the net present value (NPV). Then you just have to compare the NPVs of the three options and choose the cheapest one.

So, let's start building some spreadsheets. The contract hire spreadsheet needs to look like this:

	A	B	C	D	E	F	G	H	I
1	Contract hire								
2	Month	Opening balance	Payment	Sub-total	Interest	Closing balance			
3	1	0	=-I$3*3	=+B3+C3	=+D3*0.055/12	=+D3+E3		Rental	400
4	2	=+F3	=-I$3	=+B4+C4	=+D4*0.055/12	=+D4+E4			
5	3	=+F4	=-I$3	=+B5+C5	=+D5*0.055/12	=+D5+E5			
6	4	=+F5	=-I$3	=+B6+C6	=+D6*0.055/12	=+D6+E6			
7	5	=+F6	=-I$3	=+B7+C7	=+D7*0.055/12	=+D7+E7			
8	6	=+F7	=-I$3	=+B8+C8	=+D8*0.055/12	=+D8+E8			
9	7	=+F8	=-I$3	=+B9+C9	=+D9*0.055/12	=+D9+E9			
10	8	=+F9	=-I$3	=+B10+C10	=+D10*0.055/12	=+D10+E10			
11	9	=+F10	=-I$3	=+B11+C11	=+D11*0.055/12	=+D11+E11			
12	0	=+F11	=-I$3	=+B12+C12	=+D12*0.055/12	=+D12+E12			
13	11	=+F12	=-I$3	=+B13+C13	=+D13*0.055/12	=+D13+E13			
14	12	=+F13	=-I$3	=+B14+C14	=+D14*0.055/12	=+D14+E14			
15	13	=+F14	=-I$3	=+B15+C15	=+D15*0.055/12	=+D15+E15			
16	14	=+F15	=-I$3	=+B16+C16	=+D16*0.055/12	=+D16+E16			
17	15	=+F16	=-I$3	=+B17+C17	=+D17*0.055/12	=+D17+E17			
18	16	=+F17	=-I$3	=+B18+C18	=+D18*0.055/12	=+D18+E18			
19	17	=+F18	=-I$3	=+B19+C19	=+D19*0.055/12	=+D19+E19			
20	18	=+F19	=-I$3	=+B20+C20	=+D20*0.055/12	=+D20+E20			
21	19	=+F20	=-I$3	=+B21+C21	=+D21*0.055/12	=+D21+E21			
22	20	=+F21	=-I$3	=+B22+C22	=+D22*0.055/12	=+D22+E22			
23	21	=+F22	=-I$3	=+B23+C23	=+D23*0.055/12	=+D23+E23			
24	22	=+F23	=-I$3	=+B24+C24	=+D24*0.055/12	=+D24+E24			
25	23	=+F24	0	=+B25+C25	=+D25*0.055/12	=+D25+E25			
26	24	=+F25	0	=+B26+C26	=+D26*0.055/12	=+D26+E26			

This may look daunting but in reality you enter most items into row 4, highlight the whole row, then drag down the whole row and the remaining rows auto-populate themselves.

There are a few important things to note:

- There is no opening balance on day 1
- The first payment is 3 times the size of regular payments
- Interest (column E) is charged at the end of the month at 5.5% p.a. (i.e. 0.055 ÷ 12) on the balance that's been outstanding the whole month (column D).

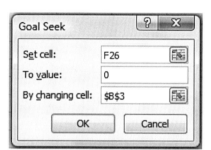

Now we use the Goal Seek function to calculate the present value.

Click on Data > What-If-Analysis > Goal Seek and enter values as shown (left).

This is the result you will get:

	A	B	C	D	E	F	G	H	I
1	Contract hire								
2	Month	Opening balance	Payment	Sub-total	Interest	Closing balance			
3	1	£9,190.98	-£1,200.00	£7,990.98	£36.63	£8,027.61		Rental	£400.00
4	2	£8,027.61	-£400.00	£7,627.61	£34.96	£7,662.57			
5	3	£7,662.57	-£400.00	£7,262.57	£33.29	£7,295.85			
6	4	£7,295.85	-£400.00	£6,895.85	£31.61	£6,927.46			
7	5	£6,927.46	-£400.00	£6,527.46	£29.92	£6,557.38			
8	6	£6,557.38	-£400.00	£6,157.38	£28.22	£6,185.60			
9	7	£6,185.60	-£400.00	£5,785.60	£26.52	£5,812.12			
10	8	£5,812.12	-£400.00	£5,412.12	£24.81	£5,436.92			
11	9	£5,436.92	-£400.00	£5,036.92	£23.09	£5,060.01			
12	0	£5,060.01	-£400.00	£4,660.01	£21.36	£4,681.37			
13	11	£4,681.37	-£400.00	£4,281.37	£19.62	£4,300.99			
14	12	£4,300.99	-£400.00	£3,900.99	£17.88	£3,918.87			
15	13	£3,918.87	-£400.00	£3,518.87	£16.13	£3,535.00			
16	14	£3,535.00	-£400.00	£3,135.00	£14.37	£3,149.36			
17	15	£3,149.36	-£400.00	£2,749.36	£12.60	£2,761.97			
18	16	£2,761.97	-£400.00	£2,361.97	£10.83	£2,372.79			
19	17	£2,372.79	-£400.00	£1,972.79	£9.04	£1,981.83			
20	18	£1,981.83	-£400.00	£1,581.83	£7.25	£1,589.08			
21	19	£1,589.08	-£400.00	£1,189.08	£5.45	£1,194.53			
22	20	£1,194.53	-£400.00	£794.53	£3.64	£798.18			
23	21	£798.18	-£400.00	£398.18	£1.82	£400.00			
24	22	£400.00	-£400.00	£0.00	£0.00	£0.00			
25	23	£0.00	£0.00	£0.00	£0.00	£0.00			
26	24	£0.00	£0.00	£0.00	£0.00	£0.00			
27			-£9,600.00						

This spreadsheet tells us that the total amount you will pay is £9,600.00, which is £9,190.98 in present value terms as shown in cell B3.

Moving on to the lease purchase option, we now need to build a similar spreadsheet, entering all of the payments into column C.

	A	B	C	D	E	F	G	H	I
29	Lease purchase								
30	Month	Opening balance	Payment	Sub-total	Interest	Closing balance			
31	1	£9,357.82	-£2,400.00	£6,957.82	£31.89	£6,989.71		Rental	£340.00
32	2	£6,989.71	-£340.00	£6,649.71	£30.48	£6,680.19			
33	3	£6,680.19	-£340.00	£6,340.19	£29.06	£6,369.25			
34	4	£6,369.25	-£340.00	£6,029.25	£27.63	£6,056.88			
35	5	£6,056.88	-£340.00	£5,716.88	£26.20	£5,743.08			
36	6	£5,743.08	-£340.00	£5,403.08	£24.76	£5,427.85			
37	7	£5,427.85	-£340.00	£5,087.85	£23.32	£5,111.17			
38	8	£5,111.17	-£340.00	£4,771.17	£21.87	£4,793.03			
39	9	£4,793.03	-£340.00	£4,453.03	£20.41	£4,473.44			
40	0	£4,473.44	-£340.00	£4,133.44	£18.94	£4,152.39			
41	11	£4,152.39	-£340.00	£3,812.39	£17.47	£3,829.86			
42	12	£3,829.86	-£340.00	£3,489.86	£16.00	£3,505.86			
43	13	£3,505.86	-£340.00	£3,165.86	£14.51	£3,180.37			
44	14	£3,180.37	-£340.00	£2,840.37	£13.02	£2,853.39			
45	15	£2,853.39	-£340.00	£2,513.39	£11.52	£2,524.91			
46	16	£2,524.91	-£340.00	£2,184.91	£10.01	£2,194.92			
47	17	£2,194.92	-£340.00	£1,854.92	£8.50	£1,863.42			
48	18	£1,863.42	-£340.00	£1,523.42	£6.98	£1,530.40			
49	19	£1,530.40	-£340.00	£1,190.40	£5.46	£1,195.86			
50	20	£1,195.86	-£340.00	£855.86	£3.92	£859.78			
51	21	£859.78	-£340.00	£519.78	£2.38	£522.17			
52	22	£522.17	-£340.00	£182.17	£0.83	£183.00			
53	23	£183.00	-£340.00	-£157.00	-£0.72	-£157.72			
54	24	-£157.72	-£340.00	-£497.72	-£2.28	-£500.00			
55			-£10,220.00						

This time, however, we leave a £500 balance in Cell F54, being the expected £8,000 sales proceeds less the £7,500 balloon rental. We can't show this as a payment in column C because all of those payments are at the start of the month and the balloon is at the end of the month. If we were to put it into column C we would get the wrong answer once we started discounting.

Note that the £500 is a negative number, reflecting the fact that the cash is actually in your pocket whereas for the majority of the contract you have been out of pocket.

You always need to be careful with signs (+ or -) in these NPV calculations. In this example I've used a minus to denote a payment. F54 is a minus because it will take a net receipt (sale proceeds less balloon) to reduce it to zero.

The Goal Seek exercise shows a net present value of £9,357.82.

So, in present value terms, the lease purchase option would cost you £9,357.82 and the contract hire option would cost you £9,190.98.

You were right: those lease purchase monthly payments are indeed lower. However, overall this option costs you more.

But not that much more.

Think again about those expected sales proceeds. You can't be sure you'll sell the car for £8,000. How confident are you about this figure? With the contract hire deal you get certainty, with the lease purchase deal you get uncertainty with a possible upside.

You can use these models and Goal Seek to help you carry out a 'fine tuning' evaluation on just this issue. Change the figure in F54 a few times to reflect different sales proceeds, then run Goal Seek and see what NPV you get.

Bet you never thought leasing maths could be so much fun!

6

USING THE PMT FUNCTION IN EXCEL TO CALCULATE A LEASE RENTAL

IN THIS CHAPTER...

- Using Excel's PMT function to calculate the monthly payment (or lease rental)

- Introduction to rate, nper, pv and fv

- A valuable leasing maths short-cut

- Annuities

There are some special functions built into Excel that make it easy to do financial calculations. The problem is, it's easy to make a mistake when using them and it's not immediately obvious when this happens. That's why I prefer to build full annuity tables in Excel so I can see every cashflow. It's much easier to spot a mistake.

Nonetheless, it's certainly much quicker to use the Excel functions if you just want to calculate, for example, a lease rental, so we can't ignore these functions. So we will now look at one of the most useful Excel functions, PMT.

And just to make sure we don't make any mistakes I'll also show you how to check the results you get.

The PMT function allows you to calculate the monthly payment (or lease rental) if you know:

1 the amount that is being financed,

2 the interest rate and

3 the number of payments.

Let's assume we want to calculate the monthly payments over two years on a non-maintenance lease where the amount financed is £20,000 and the interest rate is 7% p.a.

To start, produce a spreadsheet showing these three amounts, as shown in cells B3 to B5 (left).

Ignore everything else in the example for now.

	A	B	C	D
1	Example	1	2	3
2				
3	Amount financed	£20,000.00	£20,000.00	£20,000.00
4	Interest rate	0.07	0.07	0.07
5	Number of payments	24	24	24
6	Future value		-£5,000.00	-£5,000.00
7	Type			1
8	Monthly payment	-£895.45	-£700.76	-£696.69
9				
10				
11	Average capital balance outstanding method			
12	Interest	£1,400.00	£1,750.00	
13	Approximate rental	-£891.67	-£697.92	

In cell B8, type in "=PMT" (without the quotation marks) and you'll notice that something interesting happens. Up pops a helpful note that says "Calculates the payment for a loan based on constant payments and a constant interest rate". Which is exactly what we want to do.

If you now type in an open bracket, so that you've typed "=PMT(", you'll see that the helpful note changes, as shown below.

	A	B	E	F
1	Example	1		
2				
3	Amount financed	£20,000.00		
4	Interest rate	0.07		
5	Number of payments	24		
6	Future value			
7	Type			
8	Monthly payment	=pmt(		
9		PMT(rate, nper, pv, [fv], [type])		

You can now see three expressions; rate, nper and pv. Those expressions are Excel-speak for Interest Rate, Number of Payments and Amount Financed, respectively, and that's exactly what you've already typed in to cells A3 to B5.

Cell B4 contains 0.07, which is another way of saying 7%, so if you click on B4 the PMT function will pick up the interest rate of 7%.

This is an annual interest rate and you need a monthly rate, so type a slash symbol and the number 12, i.e. "/12" (which is Excel-speak for "divide by 12"), and then type a comma.

Note how the "nper" expression in the helpful note has changed into bold font. This is Excel's way of telling you you've moved on from entering the interest rate and are now about to enter the number of periods. You can do this by clicking cell B5 and entering a comma.

Now the "pv" is shown in bold. We've come across PV in previous chapters. PV means present value or amount financed, so you just need to click on cell B3 and the PMT function will pick this up.

Your PMT function should now be looking like this:

	A	B	E	F
1	Example	1		
2				
3	Amount financed	£20,000.00		
4	Interest rate	0.07		
5	Number of payments	24		
6	Future value			
7	Type			
8	Monthly payment	=PMT(B4/12,B5,B3		
9		PMT(rate, nper, **pv**, [fv], [type])		

When you are looking at cells B3, B4 and B5 on your screen (rather than on the black and white typeface of this book) you will see that they are outlined in different colours which match the colours of the expressions B3, B4 and B5 in cell B8. This colour coordination is another example of Excel trying to help you see what's going on.

There are a couple of extra functions in square brackets, fv and type, but we can ignore these in this example.

Now just enter a 'close brackets' sign and press Enter, and cell B8 will show your monthly payment of £895.45.

That's it, you've now taught yourself how to use the PMT function!

Now that you've set up the formula in cell B8 you can change the amount financed, interest rate and number of payments in cells B3-B5 and the revised monthly rental will appear in cell B8.

The problem is that you now have a result but can't tell if this is correct. You need a quick way to sense-check that you've calculated the right amount. So let's look again at the monthly payment of £895.45. Does that amount look right?

The easy way to find out is to do a rough calculation using the average capital balance outstanding, as follows:

Work out the rough amount of interest payable, by:

- dividing the amount financed by 2 to derive the average amount that's being financed over the period of the lease, (i.e. the average capital balance outstanding)

- multiplying the result by the annual interest rate (in this case 7%) and then

- multiplying by the number of years (in this case 2).

£20,000 ÷ 2 x 0.07 x 2 = £1,400. This is roughly the interest payable.

The financed amount of £20,000 will also be repaid over the two year period, so in total £21,400 will be repaid. Divide this by the number of months, in this case 24, and you get a monthly payment of £891.67.

This is close enough to £895.45 to make us confident that we used the PMT function correctly.

I've set up the spreadsheet to do this automatically in cells B12 and B13. The formulae are shown below. You can ignore columns C and D for now.

	A	B	C	D
1	Example	1	2	3
2				
3	Amount financed	20000	20000	20000
4	Interest rate	0.07	0.07	0.07
5	Number of payments	24	24	24
6	Future value		-5000	-5000
7	Type			1
8	Monthly payment	=PMT(B4/12,B5,B3)	=PMT(C4/12,C5,C3,C6)	=PMT(D4/12,D5,D3,D6,D7)
9				
10				
11	Average capital balance c			
12	Interest	=+B3/2*B4*2	=+((C3+C6)/2-C6)*C4*2	
13	Approximate rental	=-(+B3+B12)/B5	=-(C12+C3+C6)/C5	

Try to do this sense-check by using mental arithmetic. After a few times you'll be surprised how easy it becomes.

Leases, of course, usually have residual values (or balloon rentals for finance leases). You need to take these into account when calculating the lease rentals and you can use the PMT function to do this too.

Example 2 in the chart above shows the same lease as we had before but this time it has a residual value (Excel calls this a future value) of £5,000. You enter this into your PMT function by entering the rate, nper and pv as before.

Then, rather than closing the bracket, you insert a comma and the 'fv' in the formula becomes bold. At that point you simply click on cell C6 and close the bracket.

Excel shows the result is £700.76.

Once again we need to sense-check this to make sure we haven't made a mistake. The average capital balance outstanding on a lease is roughly the amount half-way between the amount financed and the residual value. So in this case it's £12,500. Multiply this by 7%, and multiply the result by 2 (because the lease lasts 2 years) to get the total interest payable, which in this case is £1,750.

You can use cell C12 to calculate this, as shown above. It looks a bit messy but most of this formula is working out the mid-point between the amount financed and the future value.

So the interest is £1,750 but the rentals also have to include depreciation – the difference between the PV and FV – which in this case is £15,000. So the lease rental will be roughly £1,500 + £1,750 divided by 24, i.e. £697.92.

That's close enough to £700.76 to make us confident that we used the PMT function correctly.

The average capital balance outstanding method only delivers an approximate result and that's because lease contracts are *annuities*. Each monthly payment is part-interest and part-capital, and the proportions of these in each payment will change during the life of the lease.

Most people are familiar with this idea from their own repayment mortgage: you pay equal payments, most of which goes as interest in the early years and most reduces the principal balance in later years.

Nonetheless, the average balance outstanding method is certainly good enough to allow us to sense-check the results of PMT calculations.

You'll have noticed that the PMT function has one more expression in square brackets, "type". If you enter "1" in here it will calculate the rental and will assume the lease payments are made at the start of each month. If you leave 'type' blank the function will assume the lease payments are made at the end of the month. If you decide to build this spreadsheet in Excel, you will be able to see the result of the calculation in cell D8. It shows that if the rentals are paid at the start of the month they reduce to £696.69.

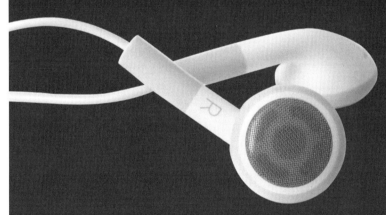

Personal

is listening to your needs.

Because we know every company is different, we offer a personal approach and packages to suit your individual business.

From simple funding to complete fleet management, we have a wide range of products and services to help make your life a little easier.

To find the right package for you, call us on **0870 333 2229** to arrange an appointment or visit **www.volkswagengroupleasing.co.uk** today.

Scan me

VOLKSWAGEN Group Leasing
Making leasing simple

7

USING THE PV FUNCTION IN EXCEL TO CALCULATE A PRESENT VALUE

IN THIS CHAPTER...

■ Introducing the Excel PV function

■ The importance of Sigma

■ Using the PV function to calculate the cheapest option

We have looked at the special function in Excel that allows you to calculate a monthly payment (or lease rental) if you know the amount that's being financed – the PMT function. And we have looked at a simple way to double-check that you've used the PMT function correctly and have arrived at the right answer. We have seen how you can use present value (PV) to compare cash flows (lease rentals, loan payments, balloon rental, residual values, etc.), and we've discussed the great benefits to be derived from using a PV approach.

In this chapter we are going to look at another Excel function, the PV function, which (surprise surprise) allows you to calculate the present value of a series of cash flows.

But first it's worthwhile dwelling for a moment on the general principles underlying all of these Excel functions, and indeed all lease v buy evaluations.

I know that some of this maths is Greek to some people (there was a time when it was Greek to me too) but now we need to introduce some real Greek into this discussion, the eighth letter of the Greek alphabet, Σ.

This letter is called Sigma and makes the same sound as the letter S. In maths we use it to mean "the sum of". So, for example, Σ 1 and 2 and 3 is 6.

In an earlier chapter we introduced this formula;

$$\frac{1}{(1 + i)^n}$$

We used this formula to calculate a discount factor, the amount by which we can discount a future payment to today's value, i.e. its PV.

The present value of a stream of future payments is the sum of those payments, after each of them has been discounted at the interest rate appropriate for the date when that future payment will take place.

That last sentence is important. We already know how to discount a future payment *at the interest rate appropriate for the date when that future payment will take place*, because the above formula allows us to calculate discount factors for each future payment. And the expression *is the sum* is relevant here because that's what the Σ does, it sums (i.e. adds together) a *stream of future payments*.

The following formula might look daunting but there's no cause for alarm as we've just described what it does.

$$PV = \sum_{1}^{36} \frac{PMT^n}{(1 + i)^n}$$

What this says is that the present value (PV) of a stream of payments (PMT) is the sum of each of those payments after it has been discounted by the discount factor appropriate for that payment.

This formula says; *start with payment 1 and discount it by $(1+i)^1$, then calculate payment 2, and discount it by $(1+i)^2$, and continue doing this until you get to payment 36 which you should discount by $(1+i)^{36}$.*

In all these cases the i is the interest rate, expressed as a decimal. So, for example, 1% per month would be entered here as 0.01.

Once you'd finished discounting all 36 payments you'd add them up to get the PV.

All of the Excel financial functions use an equation where you tell Excel some bits of information and it calculates the missing bit to make the equation balance. So when we looked at the PMT function in the last chapter we told Excel the interest rate and the PV and, because Excel holds the PMT equation, it was able to calculate the PMT.

Excel also holds the equation for the PV formula shown above. Now we are going to tell Excel the interest rate and the PMT and it is going to use the equation above to calculate the missing part, the PV.

Let's assume we want to calculate the PV of a series of lease rentals on a two year non-maintenance lease where the monthly rental is £895.45 and the annual interest rate is 7% p.a.

To start, produce a spreadsheet that looks like this.

	A	B
1	Annual interest	0.07
2	Number of payments	24
3	Rental	-895.45
4	PV	

Then, in cell B4, type in "=PV(" [without the quotation marks] and you'll notice that a helpful note pops up that looks like this:

	A	B	C	D
1	Annual interest	0.07		
2	Number of payments	24		
3	Rental	-895.45		
4	PV	=pv(		
5		PV(rate, nper, pmt, [fv], [type])		

You can now see five expressions; rate, nper, pmt, [fv] and [type]. Those expressions are Excel-speak for Interest Rate, Number of Payments (or periods), Payment Amount, Future Value and Type.

Cell B1 contains 0.07, which is another way of saying 7%, so if you click on B1 the PV function will pick up the interest rate of 7%. This is an annual interest rate and you need a monthly rate, so type a slash symbol and the number 12, i.e. "/12" (Excel-speak for "divide by 12"), and then type a comma.

The "nper" expression in the helpful note now changes into bold font, telling you you've moved on from entering the interest rate and are now about to enter the number of periods. You can do this by clicking cell B2 and entering a comma.

Now the "pmt" is shown in bold. Click on cell B3 and the function will pick this up.

If you want to you can just close the bracket now. The [fv] and [type] items are optional. If you close the bracket your spreadsheet will look like this:

	A	B	C	D
1	Annual interest	0.07		
2	Number of payments	24		
3	Rental	-895.45		
4	PV	=PV(B1/12,B2,B3)		
5		PV(rate, nper, pmt, [fv], [type])		

Press Enter and it will look like this:

	A	B
1	Annual interest	0.07
2	Number of payments	24
3	Rental	-895.45
4	PV	£19,999.96

In the last chapter we used the PMT formula to prove that the payment due on a £20,000 PV (e.g. a loan advance or lease investment) at 7% p.a. over 24 months was £895.45 per month. So now we have proved the reverse; we have used the Excel PV function to prove that the present value of 24 payments of £895.45 discounted at 7% p.a. over 24 months is £19,999.96.

The reason for the 4p difference? That's because the rental in the last chapter wasn't exactly £895.45: Excel rounded the result to the nearest penny, so in this chapter we have a small rounding difference.

You can now use this formula to your heart's content. Just change the payment (e.g. the rental), interest rate and number of payments and the formula will calculate the PV.

If your lease has a balloon rental (or a residual value) you can put this in at the [fv] stage using the same approach we went through in the last chapter.

If your lease rentals are made at the start of each month (as most are), tell Excel this by entering the number 1 into [type] in the formula and it will adjust the calculation accordingly. If you leave this blank the function will assume the lease payments are made at the end of the month.

Well done, you can now use the PV function!

So, how to use this new-found skill?

If you are offered the choice between, say, a 24 month lease with monthly payments of £300, or a 36 month lease with monthly payments of £200, you can use the PV function to calculate the PV of each of these options to help you choose the cheapest.

You'll have to decide what interest rate to use for 'i', your discount rate. Many books have been written debating the ideal number to use here. Ideally you should use your after-tax weighted average cost of capital. However, if you just want to do a quick-and-simple calculation and you normally borrow money on overdraft, just use your overdraft rate for this purpose; the result should be fine.

8

USING THE RATE FUNCTION IN EXCEL TO CALCULATE THE INTEREST RATE

IN THIS CHAPTER...

- A quick tool for lease v buy calculations.

- Comparing interest rates with lease rentals

- Why adding up the payments won't always give you the cheapest option

- Using RATE to determine the interest rate in a finance deal

If you've been following this book diligently (and hey, why wouldn't you? Doesn't everyone find maths fascinating?) you'll know we've covered quite a lot.

By now you should be able to do basic lease rental calculations and to use present value (PV) to compare cash flows.

In this chapter we will look at a quick-and-simple tool for lease v buy calculations.

If you decide to enter into a hire purchase agreement or take out a loan or use your overdraft to buy a car, the bank will tell you the interest rate.

If it's a loan regulated by the Consumer Credit Act they will give you the Annual Percentage Rate (APR). So to find the cheapest option you just need to get quotes from several lenders and compare the interest rates.

If you're considering leasing you would simply go out and get competing quotes and choose the cheapest rental.

But what if you've not decided whether you prefer a loan, hire purchase or a lease and you ask for quotes for all of them? You'll end up comparing interest rates with rentals – chalk and cheese – and you won't immediately be able to see which is the cheapest.

Let's assume you need a car costing £15,000 and that you are happy to pay something up front as a deposit. Let's also assume you're not in a small business where finance agreements are regulated by the Consumer Credit Act. After shopping around you've come up with three quotes:

- A bank will lend you £15,000 at 8% p.a. interest with 36 monthly payments of £470.05. The first payment would be due at the end of the first month of the loan.

- An HP company offers a 36 month deal with a 10% initial deposit and 36 monthly payments in advance of £426.09.

■ A leasing company offers a 3 year non-maintenance contract hire deal at £357.08 per month.

So, which is the cheapest? It's not immediately apparent, is it?

To try to work out the answer you might start by just adding up all the payments you would have to make under each of the agreements.

The totals are:

Loan	£16,921.80
HP	£15,339.20
Lease	£12,854.87

Does that mean the lease is the best deal?

Not necessarily.

As we saw earlier, just adding up the payments won't give you a good answer because this ignores the timing of those payments. It also ignores the fact that at the end of the loan and HP deals you'll be able to sell the car and recoup some of your money. And at the end of the lease you'll have to hand the car back; you don't pay for the full value of the car over three years, just the depreciation (the difference between the cost and the residual value).

So, as you can't just add up the payments, you start looking for another way to compare between them. It might be reasonable for you to ask "which of these organisations would be charging me the lowest interest rate?"

We know the bank is quoting 8% p.a. interest on the loan. At the end of the HP agreement you would own the car whereas at the end of the lease you would have to hand the car back to the leasing company. In order to compare these three options you are going to need to decide how much you think the car will be worth in three years. Let's say you decide it will be worth £5,000.

We've already looked at how to calculate the present value (PV) of a series of cash flows so you could definitely use the PV approach to work out the cheapest deal. You'd just need to calculate the PV of the cash flows for each offer and choose the one with the lowest cost net present value.

However, let's look at another way to do this sort of calculation, using Excel's RATE function. This function calculates the interest rate on a finance agreement.

To get started, set out an Excel spreadsheet like the one below. This one includes all of the things we know about so far:

■ the amount that's being financed,

■ the number of payments,

■ the monthly payment and

■ the residual value ("future value" in Excel-speak).

In Row 6 I've entered "0" to tell the RATE function that monthly payments are due at the end of the month (i.e. for the loan) and "1" where they're due at the start of the month (i.e. the HP agreement and lease).

There might be a whole range of possible payment arrangements but I've left it like this to keep the example simple.

	A	B	C	D
		Loan	Hire Purchase	Lease
1				
2	Amount financed	£15,000.00	£13,500.00	£15,000.00
3	No. of payments	36	36	36
4	Monthly payment	-£470.05	-£426.09	-£357.08
5	Future value			-£5,000.00
6	Payment timing	0	1	1
7	Interest rate			
8	Annual interest			
9				
10	Total regular payments	-£16,921.80	-£15,339.20	-£12,854.87

In row 10 I've multiplied the monthly payment amounts by the number of payments, to show the total amount payable.

The lease seems cheaper but that's mainly because of the residual value issue. And the HP deal seems cheap but we have to remember there's a 10% deposit to be paid as well as the regular payments.

We will now use the RATE function to calculate the interest rate.

Type "=rate(" into cell B7 (without the quotation marks) and Excel's ever-so-helpful reminder pops up to prompt you what to do next, as shown below.

	A	B	C	D
		Loan	Hire Purchase	Lease
1				
2	Amount financed	£15,000.00	£13,500.00	£15,000.00
3	No. of payments	36	36	36
4	Monthly payment	-£470.05	-£426.09	-£357.08
5	Future value			-£5,000.00
6	Payment timing	0	1	1
7	Interest rate	=rate(		
8	Annual interest	RATE(nper, pmt, pv, [fv], [type], [guess])		
9				
10	Total regular payments	-£16,921.80	-£15,339.20	-£12,854.87

You need to type in:

- the number of periods (nper)
- the regular payment (pmt)
- the amount advanced (pv)
- the residual value (fv)
- whether the payment is at the start or end of the month (type).

To do this click on B3 and then type a comma, B4 and comma, B2 and comma, B5 and comma and then B6 and close the brackets.

(If you're wondering, 'guess' allows you to put in a value if Excel has got confused and can't work out the right answer without a little help. Yes, really).

All being well, just before you close the bracket your spreadsheet should look like this:

	A	B	C	D
1		Loan	Hire Purchase	Lease
2	Amount financed	£15,000.00	£13,500.00	£15,000.00
3	No. of payments	36	36	36
4	Monthly payment	-£470.05	-£426.09	-£357.08
5	Future value			-£5,000.00
6	Payment timing	0	1	1
7	Interest rate	=rate(B3,B4,B2,B5,B6		
8	Annual interest	RATE(nper, pmt, pv, [fv], **[type]**, [guess])		
9				
10	Total regular payments	-£16,921.80	-£15,339.20	-£12,854.87

Once you've closed the bracket and pressed Enter you'll see an interest rate of 0.67% in cell B7 or 0.0067 if you haven't formatted this cell as a percentage. This is the 'periodic' interest rate – in this case the monthly interest rate because we're working with monthly payments.

In cell B8 you should multiply B7 by 12 to get an annual (nominal) interest rate. If we were working with quarterly payments you'd multiply by 4 instead.

If you repeat these steps for the hire purchase and lease agreements your spreadsheet will look like this:

	A	B	C	D
1		Loan	Hire Purchase	Lease
2	Amount financed	£15,000.00	£13,500.00	£15,000.00
3	No. of payments	36	36	36
4	Monthly payment	-£470.05	-£426.09	-£357.08
5	Future value			-£5,000.00
6	Payment timing	0	1	1
7	Interest rate	0.67%	0.75%	0.79%
8	Annual interest	8.00%	9.00%	9.50%
9				
10	Total regular payments	-£16,921.80	-£15,339.20	-£12,854.87

So, we can now compare the interest rates in these three deals.

HP is working out at 9% p.a. and the lease at 9.5% p.a., so the bank's offer of 8% p.a. looks good.

From which you might deduce that the loan is the best option.

The problem is, the 9.5% p.a. on the lease is only correct if your residual value estimate was correct. How confident are you that you're going to sell the car for £5,000 – net of all expenses – in three years?

Let's say that after asking around you decide you were being a bit bullish about that £5,000, and you decide that £4,450 is more likely. You can use the spreadsheet to evaluate the impact of this. Change the Future Value in D5 to £4,450 and you'll see that the interest rate changes to 7.9% p.a., making leasing the cheapest option.

	A	B	C	D
1		Loan	Hire Purchase	Lease
2	Amount financed	£15,000.00	£13,500.00	£15,000.00
3	No. of payments	36	36	36
4	Monthly payment	-£470.05	-£426.09	-£357.08
5	Future value			-£4,450.00
6	Payment timing	0	1	1
7	Interest rate	0.67%	0.75%	0.66%
8	Annual interest	8.00%	9.00%	7.90%
9				
10	Total regular payments	-£16,921.80	-£15,339.20	-£12,854.87

You needn't be concerned with how much the leasing company will pay for the car or the residual value they'll set. All that you know about the lease is that you've been quoted £357.08 per month and that this saves you having to buy the car for £15,000 and selling it for £4,450 after three years.

Armed with these three pieces of information you can fill in the data in column D and arrive at an annual interest rate that you can validly compare with the loan and HP options.

9

BRINGING TAX INTO YOUR LEASE v BUY DECISION

IN THIS CHAPTER...

- Determining the tax impact of your lease or buy decision

- Working out how tax charges and allowances affect your cash flows

- Incorporating tax cash flows into a discounting calculation

- Building a simple tax-based lease v buy evaluation

There is a tax implication to almost every investment decision you make. We can't ignore tax so in this chapter we are going to look for the first time at how to bring tax into a lease v buy analysis.

As explained in the Introduction, this book sets out to explain the underlying principles which you can apply in any country, for any kind of asset and under any set of tax rules.

To provide examples for every country, asset type or tax regime would be impossible, especially as tax rules change every year.

Therefore I am focusing on the financing of one just type of asset (motor cars) in one country (the United Kingdom) using the tax rules that were in place between 2010 and 2012.

As we make our way through the following examples I will explain the rules that applied to the financing of company cars in the UK in that period and you will be able to see how those rules affect the cash flows. To make the examples work in your country and your tax regime, for the class of assets you are interested in financing, all you need to do is to work out how your tax rules differ from the rules in the examples and change the cash flows accordingly.

In an earlier chapter we discussed the time value of money and looked at discounted cash flow analysis. We saw how Excel can be used to calculate discount factors, using the standard discounting formula:

$$\frac{1}{(1+i)^n}$$

We used Excel to produce a lease v buy analysis, in which we discounted a series of lease rentals by 1% per month.

The discounting formula was:

    $1/(1+\$A\$1)^{\wedge}1$ after 1 month

    $1/(1+\$A\$1)^{\wedge}2$ after 2 months,

    and so on.

The spreadsheet we produced is shown opposite.

The 1% per month interest rate is shown in cell A1 (as 0.01) and I've highlighted cell B5 to show how the discounting calculation worked.

The formula is repeated in cell B6, where the calculation raises the result to the power of 2 (it gets the number 2 from cell A5), and so on down column B until month 37, increasing the power by 1 each month.

This analysis compared:

■ the cost of buying a £10,000 car (including Value Added Tax) and selling it in 3 years for £2,900, against

■ simply leasing it for £259.90 per month.

As we can see, it was £69.93 cheaper (in present value terms) to lease it.

So, how would tax make this different?

Well, if you buy a car you won't be able to recover any of the VAT you pay but you will be allowed to deduct capital allowances (tax depreciation allowances) when calculating your corporation tax liability.

If you lease a car you will have to pay VAT on the rentals, only 50% of which will be recoverable against your corporation tax liability if there is any private use, and you will also get some corporation tax relief on the rentals.

Let's assume you have chosen a car emitting 95 g/km of CO_2 and that there will be some private use of the car. Let's also

	A	B	C	D	E	F
			Lease		Buy	
1	0.01		Cash flow	PV	Cash flow	PV
2						
3	Month	Discount factors				
4	1	1.00000000	-£259.90	-£259.90	-£10,000.00	-£10,000.00
5	2	=1/(1+$A$1)^A4	-£259.90	-£257.33		
6	3	0.98029605	-£259.90	-£254.78		
7	4	0.97059015	-£259.90	-£252.26		
8	5	0.96098034	-£259.90	-£249.76		
9	6	0.95146569	-£259.90	-£247.29		
10	7	0.94204524	-£259.90	-£244.84		
11	8	0.93271805	-£259.90	-£242.41		
12	9	0.92348322	-£259.90	-£240.01		
13	10	0.91433982	-£259.90	-£237.64		
14	11	0.90528695	-£259.90	-£235.28		
15	12	0.89632372	-£259.90	-£232.95		
16	13	0.88744923	-£259.90	-£230.65		
17	14	0.87866260	-£259.90	-£228.36		
18	15	0.86996297	-£259.90	-£226.10		
19	16	0.86134947	-£259.90	-£223.86		
20	17	0.85282126	-£259.90	-£221.65		
21	18	0.84437749	-£259.90	-£219.45		
22	19	0.83601731	-£259.90	-£217.28		
23	20	0.82773992	-£259.90	-£215.13		
24	21	0.81954447	-£259.90	-£213.00		
25	22	0.81143017	-£259.90	-£210.89		
26	23	0.80339621	-£259.90	-£208.80		
27	24	0.79544179	-£259.90	-£206.74		
28	25	0.78756613	-£259.90	-£204.69		
29	26	0.77976844	-£259.90	-£202.66		
30	27	0.77204796	-£259.90	-£200.66		
31	28	0.76440392	-£259.90	-£198.67		
32	29	0.75683557	-£259.90	-£196.70		
33	30	0.74934215	-£259.90	-£194.75		
34	31	0.74192292	-£259.90	-£192.83		
35	32	0.73457715	-£259.90	-£190.92		
36	33	0.72730411	-£259.90	-£189.03		
37	34	0.72010307	-£259.90	-£187.15		
38	35	0.71297334	-£259.90	-£185.30		
39	36	0.70591420	-£259.90	-£183.47		
40	37	0.69892495			£2,900.00	£2,026.88
41				-£7,903.19		-£7,973.12
42	Difference					-£69.93

assume that if you buy this car you'll get a 100% first year capital allowance (FYA) and will pay corporation tax on the car sale proceeds (the 'balancing charge'). If you lease the car you'll get 100% corporation tax relief on the lease rentals.

Remember that corporation tax rates will fall by 1% p.a. to April 2014.

We need to work out when these tax charges and allowances actually will affect your cash flows so that we can put those amounts into the discounting calculation on the correct dates. Here are four key pieces of information:

■ Capital allowances affect a company's corporation tax bill, which is paid 9 months after the company's year end.

■ VAT is accounted for on a quarterly VAT return and is payable a month later.

■ We will assume you acquire the car on 1 December 2011

■ We will assume your company's accounting year ends on 31 December and that you have calendar VAT quarters.

Armed with this information we can now put the cash flow effects of all these tax items into the discounting analysis.

The result is shown on pages 62 and 63.

As you can see, 50% of the VAT on the lease rentals will be recovered one month after the end of each VAT quarter and corporation tax relief on the lease rentals will arrive 9 months after the accounting year end.

If you decide to buy rather than lease, the 100% first year allowance will deliver a whopping 26% corporation tax benefit 9 months after the year end, and a balancing charge will eventually be payable on the car sale proceeds.

Columns J and N show how the actual cash flows have been discounted (i.e. reduced) as a result of applying the discount factors in column C.

We add up these two sets of discounted cash flows to see the cost of each option – buying and leasing – in present value terms.

This analysis shows that buying the car would be £1,038.00 cheaper than leasing it, in PV terms, which is actually the reverse of what we saw before we brought tax into the evaluation. In this situation you would therefore choose to buy rather than lease.

However, this is an extreme example and there are four reasons why it is showing that buying is cheaper than leasing:

1   The car is bought just one month before the accounting year end, so the benefit of the first year allowance cash arrives very quickly, just 10 months later. Had the car been bought just over one month later, on the first day of the new accounting year, you would have had to wait an extra 12 months for this benefit to arrive.

2   Corporation tax rates generally are falling in this analysis so the balancing charge will be taxed at only 23% whereas the first year allowance was given at 26%.

3   The lease rate was quite expensive in the first place.

4   I chose a very low emission car.

Just to reiterate: this book aims to cover the mathematics of leasing rather than any particular tax rules. Therefore my limited aspiration here has been to explain how to bring tax into a lease v buy analysis, rather than providing comprehensive details on the tax regulations.

I've made some *big* simplifying assumptions.

For example, I've used simplified tax rates and have ignored the fact that the company might have to pay interest to finance the purchase of the car. So please don't write in to say I've oversimplified the analysis – I know this already!

	A	B	C	D	E	F	G	H
1	0.01					Lease		
2-3	Month	Date	Discount factors		Rental paid	VAT paid on rental	VAT recovered on rental	Corp tax relief on lease rental
4	1	01/12/2011	1.00000000		−£259.90	−£51.98		
5	2	01/01/2012	0.99009901		−£259.90	−£51.98		
6	3	01/02/2012	0.98029605		−£259.90	−£51.98	£25.99	
7	4	01/03/2012	0.97059015		−£259.90	−£51.98		
8	5	01/04/2012	0.96098034		−£259.90	−£51.98		
9	6	01/05/2012	0.95146569		−£259.90	−£51.98	£77.97	
10	7	01/06/2012	0.94204524		−£259.90	−£51.98		
11	8	01/07/2012	0.93271805		−£259.90	−£51.98		
12	9	01/08/2012	0.92348322		−£259.90	−£51.98	£77.97	
13	10	01/09/2012	0.91433982		−£259.90	−£51.98		
14	11	01/10/2012	0.90528695		−£259.90	−£51.98		£67.57
15	12	01/11/2012	0.89632372		−£259.90	−£51.98	£77.97	
16	13	01/12/2012	0.88744923		−£259.90	−£51.98		
17	14	01/01/2013	0.87866260		−£259.90	−£51.98		
18	15	01/02/2013	0.86996297		−£259.90	−£51.98	£77.97	
19	16	01/03/2013	0.86134947		−£259.90	−£51.98		
20	17	01/04/2013	0.85282126		−£259.90	−£51.98		
21	18	01/05/2013	0.84437749		−£259.90	−£51.98	£77.97	
22	19	01/06/2013	0.83601731		−£259.90	−£51.98		
23	20	01/07/2013	0.82773992		−£259.90	−£51.98		
24	21	01/08/2013	0.81954447		−£259.90	−£51.98	£77.97	
25	22	01/09/2013	0.81143017		−£259.90	−£51.98		
26	23	01/10/2013	0.80339621		−£259.90	−£51.98		£779.70
27	24	01/11/2013	0.79544179		−£259.90	−£51.98	£77.97	
28	25	01/12/2013	0.78756613		−£259.90	−£51.98		
29	26	01/01/2014	0.77976844		−£259.90	−£51.98		
30	27	01/02/2014	0.77204796		−£259.90	−£51.98	£77.97	
31	28	01/03/2014	0.76440392		−£259.90	−£51.98		
32	29	01/04/2014	0.75683557		−£259.90	−£51.98		
33	30	01/05/2014	0.74934215		−£259.90	−£51.98	£77.97	
34	31	01/06/2014	0.74192292		−£259.90	−£51.98		
35	32	01/07/2014	0.73457715		−£259.90	−£51.98		
36	33	01/08/2014	0.72730411		−£259.90	−£51.98	£77.97	
37	34	01/09/2014	0.72010307		−£259.90	−£51.98		
38	35	01/10/2014	0.71297334		−£259.90	−£51.98		£748.51
39	36	01/11/2014	0.70591420		−£259.90	−£51.98	£77.97	
40	37	01/12/2014	0.69892495					
41	38	01/01/2015	0.69200490					
42	39	01/02/2015	0.68515337				£51.98	
43	40	01/03/2015	0.67836967					
44	41	01/04/2015	0.67165314					
45	42	01/05/2015	0.66500311				£0.00	
46	43	01/06/2015	0.65841892					
47	44	01/07/2015	0.65189992					
48	45	01/08/2015	0.64544546				£0.00	
49	46	01/09/2015	0.63905492					
50	47	01/10/2015	0.63272764					£657.55
51					−£9,356.40	−£1,871.28	£935.64	£2,253.33
52								
53	Difference							

	I	J	K	L	M	N
				Buy		
	Net cash flows	PV	Purchase price paid, incl VAT	Cash effect of capital allowances	Net cash flows	PV
	-£311.88	-£311.88	-£10,000.00		-£10,000.00	-£10,000.00
	-£311.88	-£308.79			£0.00	£0.00
	-£285.89	-£280.26			£0.00	£0.00
	-£311.88	-£302.71			£0.00	£0.00
	-£311.88	-£299.71			£0.00	£0.00
	-£233.91	-£222.56			£0.00	£0.00
	-£311.88	-£293.81			£0.00	£0.00
	-£311.88	-£290.90			£0.00	£0.00
	-£233.91	-£216.01			£0.00	£0.00
	-£311.88	-£285.16			£0.00	£0.00
	-£244.31	-£221.17		£2,600.00	£2,600.00	£2,353.75
	-£233.91	-£209.66			£0.00	£0.00
	-£311.88	-£276.78			£0.00	£0.00
	-£311.88	-£274.04			£0.00	£0.00
	-£233.91	-£203.49			£0.00	£0.00
	-£311.88	-£268.64			£0.00	£0.00
	-£311.88	-£265.98			£0.00	£0.00
	-£233.91	-£197.51			£0.00	£0.00
	-£311.88	-£260.74			£0.00	£0.00
	-£311.88	-£258.16			£0.00	£0.00
	-£233.91	-£191.70			£0.00	£0.00
	-£311.88	-£253.07			£0.00	£0.00
	£467.82	£375.84			£0.00	£0.00
	-£233.91	-£186.06			£0.00	£0.00
	-£311.88	-£245.63			£0.00	£0.00
	-£311.88	-£243.19			£0.00	£0.00
	-£233.91	-£180.59			£0.00	£0.00
	-£311.88	-£238.40			£0.00	£0.00
	-£311.88	-£236.04			£0.00	£0.00
	-£233.91	-£175.28			£0.00	£0.00
	-£311.88	-£231.39			£0.00	£0.00
	-£311.88	-£229.10			£0.00	£0.00
	-£233.91	-£170.12			£0.00	£0.00
	-£311.88	-£224.59			£0.00	£0.00
	£436.63	£311.31			£0.00	£0.00
	-£233.91	-£165.12			£0.00	£0.00
	£0.00	£0.00	£2,900.00		£2,900.00	£2,026.88
	£0.00	£0.00			£0.00	£0.00
	£51.98	£35.61			£0.00	£0.00
	£0.00	£0.00			£0.00	£0.00
	£0.00	£0.00			£0.00	£0.00
	£0.00	£0.00			£0.00	£0.00
	£0.00	£0.00			£0.00	£0.00
	£0.00	£0.00			£0.00	£0.00
	£0.00	£0.00			£0.00	£0.00
	£0.00	£0.00			£0.00	£0.00
	£657.55	£416.05		-£667.00	-£667.00	-£422.03
	-£8,038.71		-£7,100.00	£1,933.00	-£5,167.00	
		-£7,079.40				-£6,041.40
					Difference	£1,038.00

Perhaps the biggest simplifying assumption was to use a low emission car, which means that all the capital allowances are received in one amount via the 100% first year allowance. Had the car emitted say 140 g/km, it would have attracted only a 20% writing down allowance and at 170 g/km this would have been only 10%. These low levels of capital allowance would deliver small and ever-decreasing benefits over many years. In fact, someone could retire at 65 and their company would still be getting capital allowances on the first car they got when they joined the company at age 24!

The main reason for choosing a 100% first year allowance car was that we do not have enough space on the page to show the effect of writing down allowances being given over so many years.

10

CAPITAL ALLOWANCES ON COMPANY CARS – BIZARRE

IN THIS CHAPTER...

■ Making the example more complicated

■ Capital allowance calculations

■ Determining the cash flow effect of different capital allowances

We just looked at how to bring tax into a lease v buy analysis, using Excel.

We compared:

- the cost of buying a £10,000 car (incl VAT) and selling it in 3 years for £2,900, against

- simply leasing it for £259.90 per month.

We did a discounted cash flow calculation that took account of all of the relevant cash flows, including the tax cash flows.

That example assumed you had chosen a car emitting 95 g/km of CO_2, which means it attracts a 100% first year capital allowance (FYA). I made this assumption because it helped keep the example simple.

Now we are going to make the example more complicated and see how the analysis in the previous chapter would have differed had the car emitted a higher level of CO_2 and therefore attracted a lower level of capital allowances.

Here is a thumbnail sketch of the tax rules we are using:

- If your company buys a car you won't be able to recover any of the VAT you pay but you can deduct capital allowances when calculating your corporation tax liability.

- If the car emits 160g/km of CO_2 or less it is placed in the general plant and machinery pool for capital allowance purposes, which attracts a 20% p.a. writing down allowance (WDA).

- If the car has emissions in excess of 160g/km it goes into a special rate pool and attracts a 10% p.a. WDA.

So, let's assume the company buys three cars;

1 The first car emits 95 g/km of CO_2. It does not go into any pool because it attracts 100% FYA. When this car is sold the company will be taxed on the sale proceeds through a 'balancing charge'.

2 The second car emits 150g/km and attracts a 20% p.a. writing down allowance. The allowance is calculated annually on the 'reducing balance' of the pool. Sale proceeds are entered into the pool and any positive balance that then remains in the pool continues to attract WDAs at 10% p.a.

3 The third emits 170g/km and attracts a 10% writing down allowance, again on a reducing balance basis.

There will normally be other assets in the capital allowance pools so we cannot be certain exactly how much tax saving the company will obtain from either pool.

Therefore for the sake of simplicity I will assume that we just have one car in each pool and that these are the only items in each pool.

UK corporation tax rates will fall by 1% p.a. from 26% in April 2011 to 23% in April 2014. I've assumed they'll carry on at 23% forever though when doing your own analysis you might prefer to use a different assumption.

The company will get the benefit (or disadvantage) of the capital allowances (or balancing charge) when it pays its corporation tax bill 9 months after the company's year end.

We can ignore VAT as it is irrecoverable.

We will again assume that the company acquires all of the cars for £10,000 on 1 December 2011, one month before the its accounting year end, and sells them for £2,900 three years later.

Our objective is to work out the net present value of all of the various cash flows.

In the last chapter we compared leasing the car against buying it outright. The analysis showed the net present values were £7,079.40 for leasing and £6,041.40 for outright purchase, meaning that leasing was more expensive than buying. This was mainly because of the 100% first year allowance on the purchased car.

Now we will exclude the lease from the cash flow spreadsheet and just include the three purchases shown above; 100% FYA, 20% WDA and 10% WDA.

The first step is to produce a capital allowance computation showing how much the company will be able to claim by way of capital allowances to offset against its corporation tax liability in each year (see table, opposite).

Note that the sale proceeds are fully taxable on the 100% FYA car, but they simply reduce the balance in the pool (the balance available for future writing down allowances) on the other two cars.

This chart starkly shows that the company could still be receiving ever-diminishing writing down allowances some decades after the car has been sold.

When doing the maths you have to decide how many years' cash flows to include and I decided to stop at 30. To do the net present value spreadsheet accurately you have to show the cash flows arriving in the appropriate months, so I produced a 360-row spreadsheet. This is far too long to fit on the page, so I've hidden most of the months when there are no cash flows. As before I've assumed the company uses a discount rate of 1% per month for discounted cash flow calculations.

Capital allowances calculation

	Car with 100% first year allowance			Car with 20% writing down allowance			Car with 10% writing down allowance		
	b/fwd	Allowance	c/fwd	b/fwd	Allowance	c/fwd	b/fwd	Allowance	c/fwd
2011	£10,000.00	£10,000.00	£0.00	£10,000.00	£2,000.00	£8,000.00	£10,000.00	£1,000.00	£9,000.00
2012				£8,000.00	£1,600.00	£6,400.00	£9,000.00	£900.00	£8,100.00
2013				£6,400.00	£1,280.00	£5,120.00	£8,100.00	£810.00	£7,290.00
2014				£5,120.00	£1,024.00	£4,096.00	£7,290.00	£729.00	£6,561.00
2015	-£2,900.00	-£2,900.00	£0.00	£1,196.00	£239.20	£956.80	£3,661.00	£366.10	£3,294.90
2016				£956.80	£191.36	£765.44	£3,294.90	£329.49	£2,965.41
2017				£765.44	£153.09	£612.35	£2,965.41	£296.54	£2,668.87
2018				£612.35	£122.47	£489.88	£2,668.87	£266.89	£2,401.98
2019				£489.88	£97.98	£391.91	£2,401.98	£240.20	£2,161.78
2020				£391.91	£78.38	£313.52	£2,161.78	£216.18	£1,945.61
2021				£313.52	£62.70	£250.82	£1,945.61	£194.56	£1,751.04
2022				£250.82	£50.16	£200.66	£1,751.04	£175.10	£1,575.94
2023				£200.66	£40.13	£160.52	£1,575.94	£157.59	£1,418.35
2035				£13.79	£2.76	£11.03	£445.09	£44.51	£400.58

Sale proceeds £2,900

Note: b/fwd is net of sale proceeds

The result is as follows:

	A	B	C	D	E	F	G	H
4	Monthly interest rate	1%					Car with 100% first year allowance	
5	Month	Date	Discount factors		Purchase price paid, incl VAT, and sale proceeds	Cash effect of capital allowances	Net cash flows	PV
6	1	01/12/2011	1.00000000		-£10,000.00		-£10,000.00	-£10,000.00
7	2	01/01/2012	0.99009901				£0.00	£0.00
8	3	01/02/2012	0.98029605				£0.00	£0.00
9	4	01/03/2012	0.97059015				£0.00	£0.00
10	5	01/04/2012	0.96098034				£0.00	£0.00
11	6	01/05/2012	0.95146569				£0.00	£0.00
12	7	01/06/2012	0.94204524				£0.00	£0.00
13	8	01/07/2012	0.93271805				£0.00	£0.00
14	9	01/08/2012	0.92348322				£0.00	£0.00
15	10	01/09/2012	0.91433982				£0.00	£0.00
16	11	01/10/2012	0.90528695			£2,600.00	£2,600.00	£2,353.75
28	23	01/10/2013	0.80339621				£0.00	£0.00
40	35	01/10/2014	0.71297334				£0.00	£0.00
42	37	01/12/2014	0.69892495		£2,900.00		£2,900.00	£2,026.88
52	47	01/10/2015	0.63272764			-£667.00	-£667.00	-£422.03
64	59	01/10/2016	0.56151365					
76	71	01/10/2017	0.49831486					
88	83	01/10/2018	0.44222913					
100	95	01/10/2019	0.39245590					
112	107	01/10/2020	0.34828469					
124	119	01/10/2021	0.30908497					
136	131	01/10/2022	0.27429722					
148	143	01/10/2023	0.24342486					
160	155	01/10/2024	0.21602720					
172	167	01/10/2025	0.19171317					
184	179	01/10/2026	0.17013571					
196	191	01/10/2027	0.15098680					
208	203	01/10/2028	0.13399312					
220	215	01/10/2029	0.11891209					
232	227	01/10/2030	0.10552844					
244	239	01/10/2031	0.09365113					
256	251	01/10/2032	0.08311063					
268	263	01/10/2033	0.07375646					
280	275	01/10/2034	0.06545511					
292	287	01/10/2035	0.05808809					
304	299	01/10/2036	0.05155023					
316	311	01/10/2037	0.04574821					
328	323	01/10/2038	0.04059922					
340	335	01/10/2039	0.03602974					
352	347	01/10/2040	0.03197457					
364	359	01/10/2041	0.02837580					
365	Totals				-£7,100.00	£1,933.00	-£5,167.00	
366	Net Present Value							-£6,041.40

		Car with 20% writing down allowance				Car with 10% writing down allowance	
WDA	Cash effect of capital allowances	Net cash flows	PV	WDA	Cash effect of capital allowances	Net cash flows	PV
		-£10,000.00	-£10,000.00			-£10,000.00	-£10,000.00
		£0.00	£0.00			£0.00	£0.00
		£0.00	£0.00			£0.00	£0.00
		£0.00	£0.00			£0.00	£0.00
		£0.00	£0.00			£0.00	£0.00
		£0.00	£0.00			£0.00	£0.00
		£0.00	£0.00			£0.00	£0.00
		£0.00	£0.00			£0.00	£0.00
		£0.00	£0.00			£0.00	£0.00
		£0.00	£0.00			£0.00	£0.00
£2,000.00	£520.00	£520.00	£470.75	£1,000.00	£260.00	£260.00	£235.37
£1,600.00	£400.00	£400.00	£321.36	£900.00	£225.00	£225.00	£180.76
£1,280.00	£307.20	£307.20	£219.03	£810.00	£194.40	£194.40	£138.60
		£2,900.00	£2,026.88			£2,900.00	£2,026.88
£1,024.00	£235.52	£235.52	£149.02	£729.00	£167.67	£167.67	£106.09
£239.20	£55.02	£55.02	£30.89	£366.10	£84.20	£84.20	£47.28
£191.36	£44.01	£44.01	£21.93	£329.49	£75.78	£75.78	£37.76
£153.09	£35.21	£35.21	£15.57	£296.54	£68.20	£68.20	£30.16
£122.47	£28.17	£28.17	£11.05	£266.89	£61.38	£61.38	£24.09
£97.98	£22.53	£22.53	£7.85	£240.20	£55.25	£55.25	£19.24
£78.38	£18.03	£18.03	£5.57	£216.18	£49.72	£49.72	£15.37
£62.70	£14.42	£14.42	£3.96	£194.56	£44.75	£44.75	£12.27
£50.16	£11.54	£11.54	£2.81	£175.10	£40.27	£40.27	£9.80
£40.13	£9.23	£9.23	£1.99	£157.59	£36.25	£36.25	£7.83
£32.10	£7.38	£7.38	£1.42	£141.83	£32.62	£32.62	£6.25
£25.68	£5.91	£5.91	£1.01	£127.65	£29.36	£29.36	£5.00
£20.55	£4.73	£4.73	£0.71	£114.89	£26.42	£26.42	£3.99
£16.44	£3.78	£3.78	£0.51	£103.40	£23.78	£23.78	£3.19
£13.15	£3.02	£3.02	£0.36	£93.06	£21.40	£21.40	£2.55
£10.52	£2.42	£2.42	£0.26	£83.75	£19.26	£19.26	£2.03
£8.42	£1.94	£1.94	£0.18	£75.38	£17.34	£17.34	£1.62
£6.73	£1.55	£1.55	£0.13	£67.84	£15.60	£15.60	£1.30
£5.39	£1.24	£1.24	£0.09	£61.06	£14.04	£14.04	£1.04
£4.31	£0.99	£0.99	£0.06	£54.95	£12.64	£12.64	£0.83
£3.45	£0.79	£0.79	£0.05	£49.45	£11.37	£11.37	£0.66
£2.76	£0.63	£0.63	£0.03	£44.51	£10.24	£10.24	£0.53
£2.21	£0.51	£0.51	£0.02	£40.06	£9.21	£9.21	£0.42
£1.76	£0.41	£0.41	£0.02	£36.05	£8.29	£8.29	£0.34
£1.41	£0.32	£0.32	£0.01	£32.45	£7.46	£7.46	£0.27
£1.13	£0.26	£0.26	£0.01	£29.20	£6.72	£6.72	£0.21
£0.90	£0.21	£0.21	£0.01	£26.28	£6.04	£6.04	£0.17
	£1,736.97	-£5,363.03			£1,634.70	-£5,465.30	
			-£6,706.47				-£7,078.08

The discount factors have been calculated as before, so the formula in cell C7 is =1(1+SB$4)^A6.

When I dragged this formula down the spreadsheet Excel automatically calculated the appropriate discount factor for each month.

There are three important things to note:

- The cash benefits of capital allowances arrive 9 months after the year end

- A balancing charge is payable on the sale proceeds of the 100% FYA car

- The writing down allowances on the other cars continue for ages

The results are as follows:

Car	Cost to the company in Net Present Value terms
100% FYA allowance car	£6,041.40
20% WDA car	£6,706.47
10% WDA car	£7,087.08

This shows the benefit of the capital allowances very clearly. All other things being equal, if this company chose the 95g/km car rather than the 170g/km car, it would save over £1,000 in NPV terms. That's 15% of the cost of the car – a huge saving.

I stopped the analysis after 30 years even though there would still be a small unrelieved balance of capital allowance entitlement in the company's books, 27 years after the car had been sold. If you think this is a bizarre way for the government to provide tax benefits to companies, I share your view.

11

HOW TAX AFFECTS THE NPV OF LEASE CARS

IN THIS CHAPTER...

- Using Excel to produce a tax-inclusive DCF evaluation

- Walking through the evaluation, step by step

- The impact of different levels of CO_2

We just saw how capital allowances affect discounted cash flow calculations. We did a DCF analysis for a company that was about to buy three cars, emitting 95, 150 and 170 g/km of CO_2, so they would qualify for 100% first year allowances, 20% writing down allowances and 10% WDA respectively.

Now we need to decide whether the company should lease or buy these cars. We will use Excel to produce a discounted cash flow that includes the effect of taxation.

Let's assume the company has been offered a 3 year lease with monthly rentals of £259.90 commencing 1 December 2011. We will keep all of the other details the same as in the previous example. We will make some simplifying tax assumptions as we don't have the space to go into every issue in detail.

The first thing to notice is that we only have to do two DCF analyses. The 95 and 150g/km cars both qualify for full tax relief on the rentals because they both emit less than 160g/km of CO_2.

(See illustration on pages 76-77.)

We can see the rentals in column D, the VAT being paid on those rentals in column E and the timing of the 50% VAT recovery in column F.

Column G contains all of the corporation tax (CT) work. It shows the CT relief the company will receive on the rentals and on the disallowed VAT.

The company will be paying CT nine months after its year end. The tax relief on the lease payments will reduce the tax the company has to pay on its profits at that time.

The formula in cell G14 is "=-D4*0.26+(F6*0.26)", which means I took the rental paid on 1 December 2011 and multiplied it by the CT rate of 26%, and I then multiplied the disallowed input VAT by 26% because the company gets tax relief on this too.

	A	B	C	D	E	F
						Common to both leases
1	0.01					
2						
3	Month	Date	Discount factors	Rental paid	VAT paid on rental	VAT recovered on rental
4	1	01/12/2011	1.00000000	−£259.90	−£51.98	
5	2	01/01/2012	0.99009901	−£259.90	−£51.98	
6	3	01/02/2012	0.98029605	−£259.90	−£51.98	£25.99
7	4	01/03/2012	0.97059015	−£259.90	−£51.98	
8	5	01/04/2012	0.96098034	−£259.90	−£51.98	
9	6	01/05/2012	0.95146569	−£259.90	−£51.98	£77.97
10	7	01/06/2012	0.94204524	−£259.90	−£51.98	
11	8	01/07/2012	0.93271805	−£259.90	−£51.98	
12	9	01/08/2012	0.92348322	−£259.90	−£51.98	£77.97
13	10	01/09/2012	0.91433982	−£259.90	−£51.98	
14	11	01/10/2012	0.90528695	−£259.90	−£51.98	
15	12	01/11/2012	0.89632372	−£259.90	−£51.98	£77.97
16	13	01/12/2012	0.88744923	−£259.90	−£51.98	
17	14	01/01/2013	0.87866260	−£259.90	−£51.98	
18	15	01/02/2013	0.86996297	−£259.90	−£51.98	£77.97
19	16	01/03/2013	0.86134947	−£259.90	−£51.98	
20	17	01/04/2013	0.85282126	−£259.90	−£51.98	
21	18	01/05/2013	0.84437749	−£259.90	−£51.98	£77.97
22	19	01/06/2013	0.83601731	−£259.90	−£51.98	
23	20	01/07/2013	0.82773992	−£259.90	−£51.98	
24	21	01/08/2013	0.81954447	−£259.90	−£51.98	£77.97
25	22	01/09/2013	0.81143017	−£259.90	−£51.98	
26	23	01/10/2013	0.80339621	−£259.90	−£51.98	
27	24	01/11/2013	0.79544179	−£259.90	−£51.98	£77.97
28	25	01/12/2013	0.78756613	−£259.90	−£51.98	
29	26	01/01/2014	0.77976844	−£259.90	−£51.98	
30	27	01/02/2014	0.77204796	−£259.90	−£51.98	£77.97
31	28	01/03/2014	0.76440392	−£259.90	−£51.98	
32	29	01/04/2014	0.75683557	−£259.90	−£51.98	
33	30	01/05/2014	0.74934215	−£259.90	−£51.98	£77.97
34	31	01/06/2014	0.74192292	−£259.90	−£51.98	
35	32	01/07/2014	0.73457715	−£259.90	−£51.98	
36	33	01/08/2014	0.72730411	−£259.90	−£51.98	£77.97
37	34	01/09/2014	0.72010307	−£259.90	−£51.98	
38	35	01/10/2014	0.71297334	−£259.90	−£51.98	
39	36	01/11/2014	0.70591420	−£259.90	−£51.98	£77.97
40	37	01/12/2014	0.69892495			
41	38	01/01/2015	0.69200490			
42	39	01/02/2015	0.68515337			£51.98
43	40	01/03/2015	0.67836967			
44	41	01/04/2015	0.67165314			
45	42	01/05/2015	0.66500311			£0.00
46	43	01/06/2015	0.65841892			
47	44	01/07/2015	0.65189992			
48	45	01/08/2015	0.64544546			£0.00
49	46	01/09/2015	0.63905492			
50	47	01/10/2015	0.63272764			
51				−£9,356.40	−£1,871.28	£935.64
52						
53	Difference					

G	H	I	J	K	L
Leases where 100% of rental is tax deductible			Lease where 85% of rental is tax deductible		
Corp tax relief on lease rental and disallowed VAT	Net cash flows	PV	Corp tax relief on lease rental and disallowed VAT	Net cash flows	PV
	-£311.88	-£311.88		-£311.88	-£311.88
	-£311.88	-£308.79		-£311.88	-£308.79
	-£285.89	-£280.26		-£285.89	-£280.26
	-£311.88	-£302.71		-£311.88	-£302.71
	-£311.88	-£299.71		-£311.88	-£299.71
	-£233.91	-£222.56		-£233.91	-£222.56
	-£311.88	-£293.81		-£311.88	-£293.81
	-£311.88	-£290.90		-£311.88	-£290.90
	-£233.91	-£216.01		-£233.91	-£216.01
	-£311.88	-£285.16		-£311.88	-£285.16
£74.33	-£237.55	-£215.05	£63.18	-£248.70	-£225.14
	-£233.91	-£209.66		-£233.91	-£209.66
	-£311.88	-£276.78		-£311.88	-£276.78
	-£311.88	-£274.04		-£311.88	-£274.04
	-£233.91	-£203.49		-£233.91	-£203.49
	-£311.88	-£268.64		-£311.88	-£268.64
	-£311.88	-£265.98		-£311.88	-£265.98
	-£233.91	-£197.51		-£233.91	-£197.51
	-£311.88	-£260.74		-£311.88	-£260.74
	-£311.88	-£258.16		-£311.88	-£258.16
	-£233.91	-£191.70		-£233.91	-£191.70
	-£311.88	-£253.07		-£311.88	-£253.07
£857.67	£545.79	£438.49	£729.02	£417.14	£335.13
	-£233.91	-£186.06		-£233.91	-£186.06
	-£311.88	-£245.63		-£311.88	-£245.63
	-£311.88	-£243.19		-£311.88	-£243.19
	-£233.91	-£180.59		-£233.91	-£180.59
	-£311.88	-£238.40		-£311.88	-£238.40
	-£311.88	-£236.04		-£311.88	-£236.04
	-£233.91	-£175.28		-£233.91	-£175.28
	-£311.88	-£231.39		-£311.88	-£231.39
	-£311.88	-£229.10		-£311.88	-£229.10
	-£233.91	-£170.12		-£233.91	-£170.12
	-£311.88	-£224.59		-£311.88	-£224.59
£823.36	£511.48	£364.67	£699.86	£387.98	£276.62
	-£233.91	-£165.12		-£233.91	-£165.12
	£0.00	£0.00		£0.00	£0.00
	£0.00	£0.00		£0.00	£0.00
	£51.98	£35.61		£51.98	£35.61
	£0.00	£0.00		£0.00	£0.00
	£0.00	£0.00		£0.00	£0.00
	£0.00	£0.00		£0.00	£0.00
	£0.00	£0.00		£0.00	£0.00
	£0.00	£0.00		£0.00	£0.00
	£0.00	£0.00		£0.00	£0.00
	£0.00	£0.00		£0.00	£0.00
£723.30	£723.30	£457.65	£614.80	£614.80	£389.00
£2,478.66	-£7,813.38		£2,106.86	-£8,185.18	
		-£6,915.68			-£7,185.83
					-£270.15

Column H simply adds up the totals from the previous four columns to show us the net cash flows in each month.

That, of course, is not the end of the exercise because – as we know – a cashflow arriving in the near future is worth more than a cashflow arriving later, so we must use discount factors to discount (i.e. reduce) those cashflows to today's value.

I have used 1% per month as the discount rate to calculate the discount factors. After discounting all the cash flows and adding them up, we can see that the NPV of the fully tax-deductible leases is £6,915.68.

Columns J and K mirror columns G and H but in this case there is a 15% disallowance of the lease rental because the car emits more than 160g/km, so the numbers in column J are 85% of those in column G. As we can see, the net present value of the cashflows for that lease is £7,185.83.

So the effect of the 15% tax disallowance, in present value terms, is to increase the cost of the high-CO_2 car by £270.15.

Now we can work out whether the company is better off buying or leasing each of these cars.

The results of the analyses we have done so far are shown opposite.

	If the vehicles are bought		If the vehicles are leased		
CO$_2$ emissions	Capital allowances	Cost to the company in NPV terms	Tax deductible % of rental	Cost to the company in NPV terms	Difference
95 g/km	100% FYA allowance car	£6,041.40	100%	£6,915.68	£874.28
150 g/km	20% WDA car	£6,706.47	100%	£6,915.68	£209.21
170 g/km	10% WDA car	£7,087.08	85%	£7,185.83	£98.75

I can hear you saying it already; "Hold on, why is it cheaper for the company to buy these cars? Everyone always told me it's cheaper to lease than to buy!"

I'm glad you asked. There are two reasons and I'll explain these in detail in the next chapter.

For now however, we have seen how to prepare a DCF analysis that shows how the tax rules affect the cost of leasing and buying cars that emit different amounts of CO$_2$.

It is usually cheaper to lease than to buy and in the next chapter we will modify this example to prove it.

12

MORE WORK WITH DCF AND TAX

IN THIS CHAPTER...

- Re-evaluating using a lower rate of return

- Reviewing the results of our re-evaluation

- Understanding what happens when an assumption changes

In the last couple of chapters we have been looking at how taxation affects lease v buy discounted cash flow calculations.

We took an example where a company has been deciding whether to buy or lease three cars. The company could either buy the cars for £10,000 and sell them after three years for an estimated £2,900, or it could lease them for 36 monthly payments of £259.90.

The cars emit 95, 150 and 170 g/km of CO_2 respectively and if the company buys them it would be able to claim 100% first year allowances, 20% writing down allowances and 10% WDA respectively.

If the company leases the cars it will suffer a 15% disallowance on the lease rental of the 170g/km car.

Also, VAT is not recoverable on 50% of the lease rentals if the cars have any private use.

We used discounted cash flow analysis to work out whether the company would be better off buying or leasing each of these cars, and here are the results we arrived at:

CO₂ emissions	If the vehicles are bought		If the vehicles are leased		Difference
	Capital allowances	Cost to the company in NPV terms	Tax deductible % of rental	Cost to the company in NPV terms	
95 g/km	100% FYA allowance car	£6,041.40	100%	£6,915.68	£874.28
150 g/km	20% WDA car	£6,706.47	100%	£6,915.68	£209.21
170 g/km	10% WDA car	£7,087.08	85%	£7,185.83	£98.75

This chart shows that it was cheaper for the company to buy rather than lease these cars, which is not what most people expect. Indeed, it is usually cheaper to lease than to buy.

So why was it more expensive to lease in this example?

The main reason is that this particular lease is extremely expensive. Let's quickly prove that, using the shortcut described in an earlier chapter.

The leasing company is going to buy the car for £10,000 and recover 20% input VAT, bringing their net investment down to £8,333.33. (The formula to remove the VAT from the gross price is £10,000 x 100%/120%).

They will then sell the car for £2,900, of which 20% is output VAT, so they will end up with £2,416.66 net sale proceeds.

The difference between £8,333.33 and £2,416.66 is £5,916.67 and this is the depreciation the leasing company expects to suffer.

They will receive 36 rentals of £259.90, i.e. £9,356.40, and as £5,916.67 represents depreciation (repayment of the principal amount outstanding in the leasing company's books) the remaining £3,439.73 represents interest on their investment.

The average capital balance outstanding on the lease is roughly the mid-point between the £8,333.33 invested and the £2,416.66 net sale proceeds, i.e. £5,374.99. We can view this as the average amount that will be outstanding every year for 3 years.

£3,439.73 spread over 3 years is £1,146.58 per annum.

This means that effectively the leasing company will receive £1,146.58 return for an average annual investment of £5,374.99, which is a whopping 21.33% p.a. This is a very high rate and is the main reason why the lease option is more expensive than buying the car.

Let's reduce this rate now and calculate the rental assuming the leasing company requires a 6% return rather than 21.33%.

You could use a financial calculator to do this calculation but it's easy to do with a few clicks in Excel, using the Goal Seek function:

	Brought forward	Rent	Sub-total	Interest	Balance at month end		
1	8,333.33	191.12	8,142.21	40.71	8,182.92	Interest	0.50
2	8,182.92	191.12	7,991.79	39.96	8,031.75	Rental	191.12
3	8,031.75	191.12	7,840.63	39.20	7,879.83		
4	7,879.83	191.12	7,688.71	38.44	7,727.15		
5	7,727.15	191.12	7,536.03	37.68	7,573.71		
6	7,573.71	191.12	7,382.58	36.91	7,419.49		
7	7,419.49	191.12	7,228.37	36.14	7,264.51		
8	7,264.51	191.12	7,073.39	35.37	7,108.75		
9	7,108.75	191.12	6,917.63	34.59	6,952.22		
10	6,952.22	191.12	6,761.09	33.81	6,794.90		
11	6,794.90	191.12	6,603.78	33.02	6,636.79		
12	6,636.79	191.12	6,445.67	32.23	6,477.90		
13	6,477.90	191.12	6,286.77	31.43	6,318.21		
14	6,318.21	191.12	6,127.08	30.64	6,157.72		
15	6,157.72	191.12	5,966.59	29.83	5,996.43		
16	5,996.43	191.12	5,805.30	29.03	5,834.33		
17	5,834.33	191.12	5,643.21	28.22	5,671.42		
18	5,671.42	191.12	5,480.30	27.40	5,507.70		
19	5,507.70	191.12	5,316.58	26.58	5,343.16		
20	5,343.16	191.12	5,152.03	25.76	5,177.79		
21	5,177.79	191.12	4,986.67	24.93	5,011.60		
22	5,011.60	191.12	4,820.48	24.10	4,844.58		
23	4,844.58	191.12	4,653.46	23.27	4,676.72		
24	4,676.72	191.12	4,485.60	22.43	4,508.03		
25	4,508.03	191.12	4,316.90	21.58	4,338.49		
26	4,338.49	191.12	4,147.36	20.74	4,168.10		
27	4,168.10	191.12	3,976.98	19.88	3,996.86		
28	3,996.86	191.12	3,805.74	19.03	3,824.77		
29	3,824.77	191.12	3,633.64	18.17	3,651.81		
30	3,651.81	191.12	3,460.69	17.30	3,477.99		
31	3,477.99	191.12	3,286.86	16.43	3,303.30		
32	3,303.30	191.12	3,112.17	15.56	3,127.74		
33	3,127.74	191.12	2,936.61	14.68	2,951.29		
34	2,951.29	191.12	2,760.17	13.80	2,773.97		
35	2,773.97	191.12	2,582.85	12.91	2,595.76		
36	2,595.76	191.12	2,404.64	12.02	2,416.66		

As we've covered this type of spreadsheet in an earlier chapter I won't dwell on the details now.

This spreadsheet proves that if the leasing company charges 0.5% per month (i.e. 6% p.a.) for a vehicle costing £8,333.33 net of VAT, and that it expects to sell this for £2,416.66 net, it requires 36 monthly rentals of £191.12.

This is a lot cheaper than the £259.90 we were working with in the last chapter.

If we now use this new rental in our lease v buy evaluation rather than the £259.90, we get very different results (see table on pages 86-87).

We can now summarise the company's options again, this time using the net present value results we achieved using the lower rental:

	If the vehicles are bought		If the vehicles are leased		
CO_2 emissions	Capital allowances	Cost to the company in NPV terms	Tax deductible % of rental	Cost to the company in NPV terms	Difference
95 g/km	100% FYA allowance car	£6,041.40	100%	£5,043.80	-£997.60
150 g/km	20% WDA car	£6,706.47	100%	£5,043.80	-£1,662.67
170 g/km	10% WDA car	£7,087.08	85%	£5,248.72	-£1,838.38

This shows very clearly that leasing is the cheaper option than buying for all levels of CO_2 and particularly for the higher CO_2 car.

Clearly, we would get different results if we were to:

- increase the lease rate or

- alter the rental payment pattern (to, say, 3+33 rather than 1+35) or

- alter the DCF discount rate or

- change the expected sales price

And that's part of the challenge when doing these calculations – trying to work what would happen if one of your assumptions was to change and then using this spreadsheet to do 'what if' calculations to work out the effect of the change.

	A	B	C	D	E	F
1	0.01				Common to both leases	
2	Month	Date	Discount factors	Rental paid	VAT paid on rental	VAT recovered on rental
3	1	01/12/2011	1.00000000	−£191.12	−£38.22	
4	2	01/01/2012	0.99009901	−£191.12	−£38.22	
5	3	01/02/2012	0.98029605	−£191.12	−£38.22	£19.11
6	4	01/03/2012	0.97059015	−£191.12	−£38.22	
7	5	01/04/2012	0.96098034	−£191.12	−£38.22	
8	6	01/05/2012	0.95146569	−£191.12	−£38.22	£57.34
9	7	01/06/2012	0.94204524	−£191.12	−£38.22	
10	8	01/07/2012	0.93271805	−£191.12	−£38.22	
11	9	01/08/2012	0.92348322	−£191.12	−£38.22	£57.34
12	10	01/09/2012	0.91433982	−£191.12	−£38.22	
13	11	01/10/2012	0.90528695	−£191.12	−£38.22	
14	12	01/11/2012	0.89632372	−£191.12	−£38.22	£57.34
15	13	01/12/2012	0.88744923	−£191.12	−£38.22	
16	14	01/01/2013	0.87866260	−£191.12	−£38.22	
17	15	01/02/2013	0.86996297	−£191.12	−£38.22	£57.34
18	16	01/03/2013	0.86134947	−£191.12	−£38.22	
19	17	01/04/2013	0.85282126	−£191.12	−£38.22	
20	18	01/05/2013	0.84437749	−£191.12	−£38.22	£57.34
21	19	01/06/2013	0.83601731	−£191.12	−£38.22	
22	20	01/07/2013	0.82773992	−£191.12	−£38.22	
23	21	01/08/2013	0.81954447	−£191.12	−£38.22	£57.34
24	22	01/09/2013	0.81143017	−£191.12	−£38.22	
25	23	01/10/2013	0.80339621	−£191.12	−£38.22	
26	24	01/11/2013	0.79544179	−£191.12	−£38.22	£57.34
27	25	01/12/2013	0.78756613	−£191.12	−£38.22	
28	26	01/01/2014	0.77976844	−£191.12	−£38.22	
29	27	01/02/2014	0.77204796	−£191.12	−£38.22	£57.34
30	28	01/03/2014	0.76440392	−£191.12	−£38.22	
31	29	01/04/2014	0.75683557	−£191.12	−£38.22	
32	30	01/05/2014	0.74934215	−£191.12	−£38.22	£57.34
33	31	01/06/2014	0.74192292	−£191.12	−£38.22	
34	32	01/07/2014	0.73457715	−£191.12	−£38.22	
35	33	01/08/2014	0.72730411	−£191.12	−£38.22	£57.34
36	34	01/09/2014	0.72010307	−£191.12	−£38.22	
37	35	01/10/2014	0.71297334	−£191.12	−£38.22	
38	36	01/11/2014	0.70591420	−£191.12	−£38.22	£57.34
39	37	01/12/2014	0.69892495			
40	38	01/01/2015	0.69200490			
41	39	01/02/2015	0.68515337			£38.22
42	40	01/03/2015	0.67836967			
43	41	01/04/2015	0.67165314			
44	42	01/05/2015	0.66500311			£0.00
45	43	01/06/2015	0.65841892			
46	44	01/07/2015	0.65189992			
47	45	01/08/2015	0.64544546			£0.00
48	46	01/09/2015	0.63905492			
49	47	01/10/2015	0.63272764			
50				−£6,880.32	−£1,376.06	£688.03
51						
52	Difference					

G	H	I	J	K	L
Leases where 100% of rental is tax deductible			Lease where 85% of rental is tax deductible		
Corp tax relief on lease rental and disallowed VAT	Net cash flows	PV	Corp tax relief on lease rental and disallowed VAT	Net cash flows	PV
	-£229.34	-£229.34		-£229.34	-£229.34
	-£229.34	-£227.07		-£229.34	-£227.07
	-£210.23	-£206.09		-£210.23	-£206.09
	-£229.34	-£222.60		-£229.34	-£222.60
	-£229.34	-£220.40		-£229.34	-£220.40
	-£172.01	-£163.66		-£172.01	-£163.66
	-£229.34	-£216.05		-£229.34	-£216.05
	-£229.34	-£213.91		-£229.34	-£213.91
	-£172.01	-£158.85		-£172.01	-£158.85
	-£229.34	-£209.70		-£229.34	-£209.70
£54.66	-£174.68	-£158.14	£46.46	-£182.88	-£165.56
	-£172.01	-£154.17		-£172.01	-£154.17
	-£229.34	-£203.53		-£229.34	-£203.53
	-£229.34	-£201.52		-£229.34	-£201.52
	-£172.01	-£149.64		-£172.01	-£149.64
	-£229.34	-£197.55		-£229.34	-£197.55
	-£229.34	-£195.59		-£229.34	-£195.59
	-£172.01	-£145.24		-£172.01	-£145.24
	-£229.34	-£191.74		-£229.34	-£191.74
	-£229.34	-£189.84		-£229.34	-£189.84
	-£172.01	-£140.97		-£172.01	-£140.97
	-£229.34	-£186.10		-£229.34	-£186.10
£651.33	£421.99	£339.02	£553.63	£324.29	£260.53
	-£172.01	-£136.82		-£172.01	-£136.82
	-£229.34	-£180.62		-£229.34	-£180.62
	-£229.34	-£178.84		-£229.34	-£178.84
	-£172.01	-£132.80		-£172.01	-£132.80
	-£229.34	-£175.31		-£229.34	-£175.31
	-£229.34	-£173.58		-£229.34	-£173.58
	-£172.01	-£128.89		-£172.01	-£128.89
	-£229.34	-£170.16		-£229.34	-£170.16
	-£229.34	-£168.47		-£229.34	-£168.47
	-£172.01	-£125.10		-£172.01	-£125.10
	-£229.34	-£165.15		-£229.34	-£165.15
£625.28	£395.93	£282.29	£531.49	£302.14	£215.42
	-£172.01	-£121.42		-£172.01	-£121.42
	£0.00	£0.00		£0.00	£0.00
	£0.00	£0.00		£0.00	£0.00
	£38.22	£26.19		£38.22	£26.19
	£0.00	£0.00		£0.00	£0.00
	£0.00	£0.00		£0.00	£0.00
	£0.00	£0.00		£0.00	£0.00
	£0.00	£0.00		£0.00	£0.00
	£0.00	£0.00		£0.00	£0.00
	£0.00	£0.00		£0.00	£0.00
	£0.00	£0.00		£0.00	£0.00
£549.28	£549.28	£347.55	£466.89	£466.89	£295.41
£1,880.55	-£5,687.80		£1,598.47	-£5,969.88	
		-£5,043.80			-£5,248.72
					-£204.92

13

DO DISCOUNT FACTORS MAKE A DIFFERENCE?

IN THIS CHAPTER...

■ The dangers of over-simplification

■ Choosing a discount rate

■ The effect of changing the discount rate

In the last few chapters we have looked in some detail at discounted cash flow and lease v buy analysis, and we then introduced taxation to make things even more interesting.

It is fair to say that some of these issues are complex. DCF isn't the most obvious of concepts, indeed it didn't even exist as a formal method of business analysis before the 1930s. Nonetheless, it's a great tool and you can use it to perform every type of financial analysis where time is involved. For example:

■ Should you pay cash for a car or lease it?

■ Would it be cheaper to buy it on HP or lease purchase?

■ Is that finance lease deal cheaper than the contract hire deal?

DCF can handle all of these with ease.

By using Excel to do these calculations we have been able to see exactly how each number has been arrived at, which is so much more valuable than looking at the screen of a financial calculator and wondering where the result came from.

Leasing companies have special software to do these tax-based DCF calculations, which gives the right answers and shows all of the workings. You should definitely consider asking your leasing company to run an evaluation for you using this software to work out the optimum method to finance your cars, tailored to your specific circumstances.

So, back to our example. You will recall that we've been looking at a fictitious company that was deciding whether to buy or lease one of three cars. These cars all cost the same to buy or lease but had different emissions levels. The company could opt to buy for £10,000 and sell after three years for an estimated £2,900, or they could lease for 36 monthly payments of £191.12 + VAT.

When confronted with that simple choice, I suspect that most business managers would do this quick sum:

"If I buy the car it will cost me £10,000 and I'll sell it for £2,900, so the net cost is £7,100.00.

"If I lease the car it will cost me 36 x £191.12 + VAT. I can get back half of this VAT, so leasing ends up costing me £7,568.35.

"Therefore I'll buy the car, it's a lot cheaper."

From the work we did in the last chapter we know that this is a massive over-simplification. In fact the answer is plain wrong, because it ignores corporation (or income) tax, CO_2 emissions and discount rates.

After taking those three factors into consideration we got these results:

	If the vehicles are bought		If the vehicles are leased		
CO_2 emissions	Capital allowances	Cost to the company in NPV terms	Tax deductible % of rental	Cost to the company in NPV terms	Difference
95 g/km	100% FYA allowance car	£6,041.40	100%	£5,043.80	-£997.60
150 g/km	20% WDA car	£6,706.47	100%	£5,043.80	-£1,662.67
170 g/km	10% WDA car	£7,087.08	85%	£5,248.72	-£1,838.38

So it turned out that leasing was a lot cheaper than buying.

We now need to revisit that word 'discounting'. We have discussed tax in some detail but have not spent much time considering the choice of discount rate.

So far we've used a discount rate of 1% per month, i.e. 12% p.a., for all of these calculations, and I chose this because it's then very simple to see how the calculation works on the spreadsheet. 1% of any number can be spotted a mile away.

But now is time to ask the question, how would our results differ if we changed the discount rate?

In fact, how do we decide what discount rate to use anyway?

There has been a huge amount of academic discussion over the years on how to select the right discount rate. Books have been written about this. Should we use pre-tax borrowing cost? Post-tax borrowing cost? Incremental borrowing cost? There are lots of opinions.

If you are keen to find out more about this, look up 'cost of capital', 'weighted average cost of capital' or 'Modigliani v Miller' on Google.

Mercifully, that topic is *way* beyond the brief of this book, so my suggestion is that you simply try to find a discount rate that makes sense to your business without over-complicating things.

For example, if you are cash-rich and will be using money from your deposit account to pay for the car or the lease rentals, simply use your deposit account interest rate as your DCF discounting rate.

Or if you have an overdraft and would use it to buy the car or pay the lease rentals, use your overdraft interest rate.

Yes, these rates will change over time but you have to start somewhere and I do want to keep the next example simple!

So, let's say that you use your overdraft constantly and that it costs you 2.5% over bank base rate, i.e. 3% p.a.

Turning now to the spreadsheet we produced a few chapters ago, where we showed the NPV of *buying* the three cars, all we have to do now is to change the discount rate in cell B4 from 1% per month (i.e. 12% p.a.) to 0.25% per month (i.e. 3% p.a.) and we find that we have changed the difference in NPV between these cars quite dramatically.

Monthly interest rate	0.25%	cell B4			Car with 100% first year allowance		
Month	Date	Discount factors	Purchase price paid, incl VAT, and sale proceeds	Cash effect of capital allowances		Net cash flows	PV
1	01/12/2011	1.00000000	−£10,000.00			−£10,000.00	−£10,000.00
2	01/01/2012	0.99750623				£0.00	£0.00
3	01/02/2012	0.99501869				£0.00	£0.00
4	01/03/2012	0.99253734				£0.00	£0.00
5	01/04/2012	0.99006219				£0.00	£0.00
6	01/05/2012	0.98759321				£0.00	£0.00
7	01/06/2012	0.98513038				£0.00	£0.00
8	01/07/2012	0.98267370				£0.00	£0.00
9	01/08/2012	0.98022314				£0.00	£0.00
10	01/09/2012	0.97777869				£0.00	£0.00
11	01/10/2012	0.97534034		£2,600.00		£2,600.00	£2,535.88
23	01/10/2013	0.94655011				£0.00	£0.00
35	01/10/2014	0.91860972				£0.00	£0.00
37	01/12/2014	0.91403384	£2,900.00			£2,900.00	£2,650.70
47	01/10/2015	0.89149407		−£667.00		−£667.00	−£594.63
59	01/10/2016	0.86517883					
71	01/10/2017	0.83964037					
83	01/10/2018	0.81485575					
95	01/10/2019	0.79080273					
107	01/10/2020	0.76745971					
119	01/10/2021	0.74480573					
131	01/10/2022	0.72282045					
143	01/10/2023	0.70148414					
155	01/10/2024	0.68077764					
167	01/10/2025	0.66068235					
179	01/10/2026	0.64118024					
191	01/10/2027	0.62225380					
203	01/10/2028	0.60388602					
215	01/10/2029	0.58606044					
227	01/10/2030	0.56876102					
239	01/10/2031	0.55197226					
251	01/10/2032	0.53567907					
263	01/10/2033	0.51986682					
275	01/10/2034	0.50452132					
287	01/10/2035	0.48962879					
299	01/10/2036	0.47517587					
311	01/10/2037	0.46114956					
323	01/10/2038	0.44753729					
335	01/10/2039	0.43432682					
347	01/10/2040	0.42150630					
359	01/10/2041	0.40906422					
Totals			−£7,100.00	£1,933.00		−£5,167.00	
Net Present Value							−£5,408.04

You can download all the spreadsheets in this book at www.tourick.com

Car with 20% writing down allowance				Car with 10% writing down allowance			
WDA	Cash effect of capital allowances	Net cash flows	PV	WDA	Cash effect of capital allowances	Net cash flows	PV
		-£10,000.00	-£10,000.00			-£10,000.00	-£10,000.00
		£0.00	£0.00			£0.00	£0.00
		£0.00	£0.00			£0.00	£0.00
		£0.00	£0.00			£0.00	£0.00
		£0.00	£0.00			£0.00	£0.00
		£0.00	£0.00			£0.00	£0.00
		£0.00	£0.00			£0.00	£0.00
		£0.00	£0.00			£0.00	£0.00
		£0.00	£0.00			£0.00	£0.00
£2,000.00	£520.00	£520.00	£507.18	£1,000.00	£260.00	£260.00	£253.59
£1,600.00	£400.00	£400.00	£378.62	£900.00	£225.00	£225.00	£212.97
£1,280.00	£307.20	£307.20	£282.20	£810.00	£194.40	£194.40	£178.58
		£2,900.00	£2,650.70			£2,900.00	£2,650.70
£1,024.00	£235.52	£235.52	£209.96	£729.00	£167.67	£167.67	£149.48
£239.20	£55.02	£55.02	£47.60	£366.10	£84.20	£84.20	£72.85
£191.36	£44.01	£44.01	£36.95	£329.49	£75.78	£75.78	£63.63
£153.09	£35.21	£35.21	£28.69	£296.54	£68.20	£68.20	£55.58
£122.47	£28.17	£28.17	£22.28	£266.89	£61.38	£61.38	£48.54
£97.98	£22.53	£22.53	£17.29	£240.20	£55.25	£55.25	£42.40
£78.38	£18.03	£18.03	£13.43	£216.18	£49.72	£49.72	£37.03
£62.70	£14.42	£14.42	£10.42	£194.56	£44.75	£44.75	£32.35
£50.16	£11.54	£11.54	£8.09	£175.10	£40.27	£40.27	£28.25
£40.13	£9.23	£9.23	£6.28	£157.59	£36.25	£36.25	£24.68
£32.10	£7.38	£7.38	£4.88	£141.83	£32.62	£32.62	£21.55
£25.68	£5.91	£5.91	£3.79	£127.65	£29.36	£29.36	£18.82
£20.55	£4.73	£4.73	£2.94	£114.89	£26.42	£26.42	£16.44
£16.44	£3.78	£3.78	£2.28	£103.40	£23.78	£23.78	£14.36
£13.15	£3.02	£3.02	£1.77	£93.06	£21.40	£21.40	£12.54
£10.52	£2.42	£2.42	£1.38	£83.75	£19.26	£19.26	£10.96
£8.42	£1.94	£1.94	£1.07	£75.38	£17.34	£17.34	£9.57
£6.73	£1.55	£1.55	£0.83	£67.84	£15.60	£15.60	£8.36
£5.39	£1.24	£1.24	£0.64	£61.06	£14.04	£14.04	£7.30
£4.31	£0.99	£0.99	£0.50	£54.95	£12.64	£12.64	£6.38
£3.45	£0.79	£0.79	£0.39	£49.45	£11.37	£11.37	£5.57
£2.76	£0.63	£0.63	£0.30	£44.51	£10.24	£10.24	£4.86
£2.21	£0.51	£0.51	£0.23	£40.06	£9.21	£9.21	£4.25
£1.76	£0.41	£0.41	£0.18	£36.05	£8.29	£8.29	£3.71
£1.41	£0.32	£0.32	£0.14	£32.45	£7.46	£7.46	£3.24
£1.13	£0.26	£0.26	£0.11	£29.20	£6.72	£6.72	£2.83
£0.90	£0.21	£0.21	£0.09	£26.28	£6.04	£6.04	£2.47
	£1,736.97	-£5,363.03			£1,634.70	-£5,465.30	
			-£5,758.78				-£5,996.16

If we do exactly the same to the NPV spreadsheet we prepared for the *leases*, in this case changing the interest rate in cell A101 to 0.25% per month, we get these new results:

		cell B4		Common to both leases	
0.25%					
Month	Date	Discount factors	Rental paid	VAT paid on rental	VAT recovered on rental
1	01/12/2011	1.00000000	−£191.12	−£38.22	
2	01/01/2012	0.99750623	−£191.12	−£38.22	
3	01/02/2012	0.99501869	−£191.12	−£38.22	£19.11
4	01/03/2012	0.99253734	−£191.12	−£38.22	
5	01/04/2012	0.99006219	−£191.12	−£38.22	
6	01/05/2012	0.98759321	−£191.12	−£38.22	£57.34
7	01/06/2012	0.98513038	−£191.12	−£38.22	
8	01/07/2012	0.98267370	−£191.12	−£38.22	
9	01/08/2012	0.98022314	−£191.12	−£38.22	£57.34
10	01/09/2012	0.97777869	−£191.12	−£38.22	
11	01/10/2012	0.97534034	−£191.12	−£38.22	
12	01/11/2012	0.97290807	−£191.12	−£38.22	£57.34
13	01/12/2012	0.97048187	−£191.12	−£38.22	
14	01/01/2013	0.96806171	−£191.12	−£38.22	
15	01/02/2013	0.96564759	−£191.12	−£38.22	£57.34
16	01/03/2013	0.96323949	−£191.12	−£38.22	
17	01/04/2013	0.96083740	−£191.12	−£38.22	
18	01/05/2013	0.95844130	−£191.12	−£38.22	£57.34
19	01/06/2013	0.95605117	−£191.12	−£38.22	
20	01/07/2013	0.95366700	−£191.12	−£38.22	
21	01/08/2013	0.95128878	−£191.12	−£38.22	£57.34
22	01/09/2013	0.94891649	−£191.12	−£38.22	
23	01/10/2013	0.94655011	−£191.12	−£38.22	
24	01/11/2013	0.94418964	−£191.12	−£38.22	£57.34
25	01/12/2013	0.94183505	−£191.12	−£38.22	
26	01/01/2014	0.93948634	−£191.12	−£38.22	
27	01/02/2014	0.93714348	−£191.12	−£38.22	£57.34
28	01/03/2014	0.93480646	−£191.12	−£38.22	
29	01/04/2014	0.93247527	−£191.12	−£38.22	
30	01/05/2014	0.93014990	−£191.12	−£38.22	£57.34
31	01/06/2014	0.92783032	−£191.12	−£38.22	
32	01/07/2014	0.92551653	−£191.12	−£38.22	
33	01/08/2014	0.92320851	−£191.12	−£38.22	£57.34
34	01/09/2014	0.92090624	−£191.12	−£38.22	
35	01/10/2014	0.91860972	−£191.12	−£38.22	
36	01/11/2014	0.91631892	−£191.12	−£38.22	£57.34
37	01/12/2014	0.91403384			
38	01/01/2015	0.91175445			
39	01/02/2015	0.90948075			£38.22
40	01/03/2015	0.90721272			
41	01/04/2015	0.90495034			
42	01/05/2015	0.90269361			£0.00
43	01/06/2015	0.90044250			
44	01/07/2015	0.89819701			
45	01/08/2015	0.89595712			£0.00
46	01/09/2015	0.89372281			
47	01/10/2015	0.89149407			
			−£6,880.32	−£1,376.06	£688.03

Difference

Leases where 100% of rental is tax deductible			Lease where 85% of rental is tax deductible		
Corp tax relief on lease rental and disallowed VAT	Net cash flows	PV	Corp tax relief on lease rental and disallowed VAT	Net cash flows	PV
	-£229.34	-£229.34		-£229.34	-£229.34
	-£229.34	-£228.77		-£229.34	-£228.77
	-£210.23	-£209.18		-£210.23	-£209.18
	-£229.34	-£227.63		-£229.34	-£227.63
	-£229.34	-£227.06		-£229.34	-£227.06
	-£172.01	-£169.87		-£172.01	-£169.87
	-£229.34	-£225.93		-£229.34	-£225.93
	-£229.34	-£225.37		-£229.34	-£225.37
	-£172.01	-£168.61		-£172.01	-£168.61
	-£229.34	-£224.25		-£229.34	-£224.25
£54.66	-£174.68	-£170.38	£46.46	-£182.88	-£178.37
	-£172.01	-£167.35		-£172.01	-£167.35
	-£229.34	-£222.57		-£229.34	-£222.57
	-£229.34	-£222.02		-£229.34	-£222.02
	-£172.01	-£166.10		-£172.01	-£166.10
	-£229.34	-£220.91		-£229.34	-£220.91
	-£229.34	-£220.36		-£229.34	-£220.36
	-£172.01	-£164.86		-£172.01	-£164.86
	-£229.34	-£219.26		-£229.34	-£219.26
	-£229.34	-£218.72		-£229.34	-£218.72
	-£172.01	-£163.63		-£172.01	-£163.63
	-£229.34	-£217.63		-£229.34	-£217.63
£651.33	£421.99	£399.43	£553.63	£324.29	£306.95
	-£172.01	-£162.41		-£172.01	-£162.41
	-£229.34	-£216.00		-£229.34	-£216.00
	-£229.34	-£215.47		-£229.34	-£215.47
	-£172.01	-£161.20		-£172.01	-£161.20
	-£229.34	-£214.39		-£229.34	-£214.39
	-£229.34	-£213.86		-£229.34	-£213.86
	-£172.01	-£159.99		-£172.01	-£159.99
	-£229.34	-£212.79		-£229.34	-£212.79
	-£229.34	-£212.26		-£229.34	-£212.26
	-£172.01	-£158.80		-£172.01	-£158.80
	-£229.34	-£211.20		-£229.34	-£211.20
£625.28	£395.93	£363.71	£531.49	£302.14	£277.55
	-£172.01	-£157.61		-£172.01	-£157.61
	£0.00	£0.00		£0.00	£0.00
	£0.00	£0.00		£0.00	£0.00
	£38.22	£34.76		£38.22	£34.76
	£0.00	£0.00		£0.00	£0.00
	£0.00	£0.00		£0.00	£0.00
	£0.00	£0.00		£0.00	£0.00
	£0.00	£0.00		£0.00	£0.00
	£0.00	£0.00		£0.00	£0.00
	£0.00	£0.00		£0.00	£0.00
	£0.00	£0.00		£0.00	£0.00
£549.28	£549.28	£489.68	£466.89	£466.89	£416.23
£1,880.55	-£5,687.80		£1,598.47	-£5,969.88	
		-£5,518.22			-£5,778.31
					-£260.08

If we now redo our summary we find that there have been massive changes compared with the results we saw in the last chapter:

CO₂ emissions	If the vehicles are bought		If the vehicles are leased		Difference
	Capital allowances	Cost to the company in NPV terms	Tax deductible % of rental	Cost to the company in NPV terms	
95 g/km	100% FYA allowance car	£5,408.04	100%	£5,518.22	£110.18
150 g/km	20% WDA car	£5,758.78	100%	£5,518.22	-£240.56
170 g/km	10% WDA car	£5,996.16	85%	£5,778.31	-£217.85

But hang on a moment. In the last chapter we showed that it was much cheaper (in DCF terms) to lease all of these cars rather than buy them. In this chapter we've changed just one thing – the discount rate – and the results are totally different. And it seems it's actually cheaper to buy the lowest emission car than to lease it. Why is that?

All will be revealed in the next chapter.

14

DISCOUNT FACTORS MAKE A BIG DIFFERENCE!

IN THIS CHAPTER...

- Understanding why discount rates are so important

- Re-evaluating the lease and purchase decision with different discount rates

- Cash inflows and outflows: getting the signs right

We ended the last chapter on a cliff-hanger. We had been building up a tax-based lease v buy analysis for three cars with different emissions levels, using a 1% per month (12% p.a.) discount rate, and this was the result:

| CO₂ emissions | If the vehicles are bought | | If the vehicles are leased | | Difference |
	Capital allowances	Cost to the company in NPV terms	Tax deductible % of rental	Cost to the company in NPV terms	
95 g/km	100% FYA allowance car	£6,041.40	100%	£5,043.80	-£997.60
150 g/km	20% WDA car	£6,706.47	100%	£5,043.80	-£1662.67
170 g/km	10% WDA car	£7,087.08	85%	£5,248.72	-£1838.38

Then we reduced the discount rate to 0.25% per month (3% p.a.) and re-ran the evaluations. The results were completely different.

| CO₂ emissions | If the vehicles are bought | | If the vehicles are leased | | Difference |
	Capital allowances	Cost to the company in NPV terms	Tax deductible % of rental	Cost to the company in NPV terms	
95 g/km	100% FYA allowance car	£5,408.04	100%	£5,518.22	£110.18
150 g/km	20% WDA car	£5,758.78	100%	£5,518.22	-£240.56
170 g/km	10% WDA car	£5,996.16	85%	£5,778.31	-£217.85

And the question I asked at the end of the last chapter was, quite simply, why?

First let's look at what's happened.

We didn't change a single element of the actual transactions. In the second evaluation the cars cost the same, the lease rentals were the same, the lease periods were the same and the CO_2 levels were the same. We changed only one number, the discount rate.

With a discount rate of 12% p.a. it had been £997.60 cheaper, in present value terms, to lease the lowest emission car rather than buying it. But with a discount rate of 3% p.a. it became £110.18 more expensive to lease rather than buy.

Let's look at the Excel spreadsheets and see how this happened. On the next two pages (100-101) you'll find the 12% spreadsheet that looked at buying the cars.

Below it is the first part of the 3% spreadsheet. (I've left out the rest to save space).

Have a look at those discount factors in column C. Note how quickly they decline from C6 to C16 in the 12% spreadsheet (the top spreadhseet). They're down to 0.905 (90.5%) by C16 in that spreadsheet but down to only 0.975 (97.5%) at the same stage of the 2nd spreadsheet. That's a whopping 7% difference, so when that discount rate is used to discount the benefit of the £2,600 capital allowance cash inflow on month 11, the discounted value in the first spreadsheet is £2,353.75 whereas in the second spreadsheet the much lower discount rate delivers a PV of £2,535.88.

This means that the £2,600 capital allowance has barely been discounted at all, so it's worth more to us.

By the time we've got to month 37 the difference between the discount factors in C42 in the two spreadsheets is massive. So

	A	B	C	D	E	F	G	H
4	Monthly interest rate	1.00%					Car with 100% first year allowance	
5	Month	Date	Discount factors		Purchase price paid, incl VAT, and sale proceeds	Cash effect of capital allowances	Net cash flows	PV
6	1	01/12/2011	1.00000000		−£10,000.00		−£10,000.00	−£10,000.00
7	2	01/01/2012	0.99009901				£0.00	£0.00
8	3	01/02/2012	0.98029605				£0.00	£0.00
9	4	01/03/2012	0.97059015				£0.00	£0.00
10	5	01/04/2012	0.96098034				£0.00	£0.00
11	6	01/05/2012	0.95146569				£0.00	£0.00
12	7	01/06/2012	0.94204524				£0.00	£0.00
13	8	01/07/2012	0.93271805				£0.00	£0.00
14	9	01/08/2012	0.92348322				£0.00	£0.00
15	10	01/09/2012	0.91433982				£0.00	£0.00
16	11	01/10/2012	0.90528695			£2,600.00	£2,600.00	£2,353.75
28	23	01/10/2013	0.80339621				£0.00	£0.00
40	35	01/10/2014	0.71297334				£0.00	£0.00
42	37	01/12/2014	0.69892495		£2,900.00		£2,900.00	£2,026.88
52	47	01/10/2015	0.63272764			−£667.00	−£667.00	−£422.03
64	59	01/10/2016	0.56151365					
76	71	01/10/2017	0.49831486					
88	83	01/10/2018	0.44222913					
100	95	01/10/2019	0.39245590					
112	107	01/10/2020	0.34828469					
124	119	01/10/2021	0.30908497					
136	131	01/10/2022	0.27429722					
148	143	01/10/2023	0.24342486					
160	155	01/10/2024	0.21602720					
172	167	01/10/2025	0.19171317					
184	179	01/10/2026	0.17013571					
196	191	01/10/2027	0.15098680					
208	203	01/10/2028	0.13399312					
220	215	01/10/2029	0.11891209					
232	227	01/10/2030	0.10552844					
244	239	01/10/2031	0.09365113					
256	251	01/10/2032	0.08311063					
268	263	01/10/2033	0.07375646					
280	275	01/10/2034	0.06545511					
292	287	01/10/2035	0.05808809					
304	299	01/10/2036	0.05155023					
316	311	01/10/2037	0.04574821					
328	323	01/10/2038	0.04059922					
340	335	01/10/2039	0.03602974					
352	347	01/10/2040	0.03197457					
364	359	01/10/2041	0.02837580					
365	Totals				−£7,100.00	£1,933.00	−£5,167.00	
366	Net Present Value							−£6,041.40

	A	B	C	D	E	F	G	H
4	Monthly interest rate	0.25%					Car with 100% first year allowance	
5	Month	Date	Discount factors		Purchase price paid, incl VAT, and sale proceeds	Cash effect of capital allowances	Net cash flows	PV
6	1	01/12/2011	1.00000000		−£10,000.00		−£10,000.00	−£10,000.00
7	2	01/01/2012	0.99750623				£0.00	£0.00
8	3	01/02/2012	0.99501869				£0.00	£0.00
9	4	01/03/2012	0.99253734				£0.00	£0.00
10	5	01/04/2012	0.99006219				£0.00	£0.00
11	6	01/05/2012	0.98759321				£0.00	£0.00
12	7	01/06/2012	0.98513038				£0.00	£0.00
13	8	01/07/2012	0.98267370				£0.00	£0.00
14	9	01/08/2012	0.98022314				£0.00	£0.00
15	10	01/09/2012	0.97777869				£0.00	£0.00
16	11	01/10/2012	0.97534034			£2,600.00	£2,600.00	£2,535.88
28	23	01/10/2013	0.94655011				£0.00	£0.00
40	35	01/10/2014	0.91860972				£0.00	£0.00
42	37	01/12/2014	0.91403384		£2,900.00		£2,900.00	£2,650.70
52	47	01/10/2015	0.89149407			−£667.00	−£667.00	−£594.63
364	359	01/10/2041	0.40906422					
365	Totals				−£7,100.00	£1,933.00	−£5,167.00	
366	Net Present Value							−£5,408.04

I	J	K	L	M	N	O	P

First table

	Car with 20% writing down allowance				Car with 10% writing down allowance		
WDA	Cash effect of capital allowances	Net cash flows	PV	WDA	Cash effect of capital allowances	Net cash flows	PV
		−£10,000.00	−£10,000.00			−£10,000.00	−£10,000.00
		£0.00	£0.00			£0.00	£0.00
		£0.00	£0.00			£0.00	£0.00
		£0.00	£0.00			£0.00	£0.00
		£0.00	£0.00			£0.00	£0.00
		£0.00	£0.00			£0.00	£0.00
		£0.00	£0.00			£0.00	£0.00
		£0.00	£0.00			£0.00	£0.00
		£0.00	£0.00			£0.00	£0.00
		£0.00	£0.00			£0.00	£0.00
£2,000.00	£520.00	£520.00	£470.75	£1,000.00	£260.00	£260.00	£235.37
£1,600.00	£400.00	£400.00	£321.36	£900.00	£225.00	£225.00	£180.76
£1,280.00	£307.20	£307.20	£219.03	£810.00	£194.40	£194.40	£138.60
		£2,900.00	£2,026.88			£2,900.00	£2,026.88
£1,024.00	£235.52	£235.52	£149.02	£729.00	£167.67	£167.67	£106.09
£239.20	£55.02	£55.02	£30.89	£366.10	£84.20	£84.20	£47.28
£191.36	£44.01	£44.01	£21.93	£329.49	£75.78	£75.78	£37.76
£153.09	£35.21	£35.21	£15.57	£296.54	£68.20	£68.20	£30.16
£122.47	£28.17	£28.17	£11.05	£266.89	£61.38	£61.38	£24.09
£97.98	£22.53	£22.53	£7.85	£240.20	£55.25	£55.25	£19.24
£78.38	£18.03	£18.03	£5.57	£216.18	£49.72	£49.72	£15.37
£62.70	£14.42	£14.42	£3.96	£194.56	£44.75	£44.75	£12.27
£50.16	£11.54	£11.54	£2.81	£175.10	£40.27	£40.27	£9.80
£40.13	£9.23	£9.23	£1.99	£157.59	£36.25	£36.25	£7.83
£32.10	£7.38	£7.38	£1.42	£141.83	£32.62	£32.62	£6.25
£25.68	£5.91	£5.91	£1.01	£127.65	£29.36	£29.36	£5.00
£20.55	£4.73	£4.73	£0.71	£114.89	£26.42	£26.42	£3.99
£16.44	£3.78	£3.78	£0.51	£103.40	£23.78	£23.78	£3.19
£13.15	£3.02	£3.02	£0.36	£93.06	£21.40	£21.40	£2.55
£10.52	£2.42	£2.42	£0.26	£83.75	£19.26	£19.26	£2.03
£8.42	£1.94	£1.94	£0.18	£75.38	£17.34	£17.34	£1.62
£6.73	£1.55	£1.55	£0.13	£67.84	£15.60	£15.60	£1.30
£5.39	£1.24	£1.24	£0.09	£61.06	£14.04	£14.04	£1.04
£4.31	£0.99	£0.99	£0.06	£54.95	£12.64	£12.64	£0.83
£3.45	£0.79	£0.79	£0.05	£49.45	£11.37	£11.37	£0.66
£2.76	£0.63	£0.63	£0.03	£44.51	£10.24	£10.24	£0.53
£2.21	£0.51	£0.51	£0.02	£40.06	£9.21	£9.21	£0.42
£1.76	£0.41	£0.41	£0.02	£36.05	£8.29	£8.29	£0.34
£1.41	£0.32	£0.32	£0.01	£32.45	£7.46	£7.46	£0.27
£1.13	£0.26	£0.26	£0.01	£29.20	£6.72	£6.72	£0.21
£0.90	£0.21	£0.21	£0.01	£26.28	£6.04	£6.04	£0.17
	£1,736.97	−£5,363.03			£1,634.70	−£5,465.30	
			−£6,706.47				−£7,078.08

Second table

	Car with 20% writing down allowance				Car with 10% writing down allowance		
WDA	Cash effect of capital allowances	Net cash flows	PV	WDA	Cash effect of capital allowances	Net cash flows	PV
		−£10,000.00	−£10,000.00			−£10,000.00	−£10,000.00
		£0.00	£0.00			£0.00	£0.00
		£0.00	£0.00			£0.00	£0.00
		£0.00	£0.00			£0.00	£0.00
		£0.00	£0.00			£0.00	£0.00
		£0.00	£0.00			£0.00	£0.00
		£0.00	£0.00			£0.00	£0.00
		£0.00	£0.00			£0.00	£0.00
		£0.00	£0.00			£0.00	£0.00
		£0.00	£0.00			£0.00	£0.00
£2,000.00	£520.00	£520.00	£507.18	£1,000.00	£260.00	£260.00	£253.59
£1,600.00	£400.00	£400.00	£378.62	£900.00	£225.00	£225.00	£212.97
£1,280.00	£307.20	£307.20	£282.20	£810.00	£194.40	£194.40	£178.58
		£2,900.00	£2,650.70			£2,900.00	£2,650.70
£1,024.00	£235.52	£235.52	£209.96	£729.00	£167.67	£167.67	£149.48
£239.20	£55.02	£55.02	£47.60	£366.10	£84.20	£84.20	£72.85
	£1,736.97	−£5,363.03			£1,634.70	−£5,465.30	
			−£5,758.78				−£5,996.16

when the sale proceeds of the car arrive (cell E42) in that month, they are worth much more in present value terms in the second spreadsheet, when the discount rate is low.

This same general principle applies to the purchase of the two higher-CO_2 cars as well. The benefits of the future capital allowances and the sale proceeds are more valuable to the company where the discount rate is lower, and this reduces the net cost of buying the car.

It remains the case that the higher CO_2 car is more expensive in PV terms than the lower CO_2 car but the reduction of the discount rate serves to reduce the overall cost regardless of the CO_2 rates.

We have a completely different scenario when it comes to the leases. On pages 104-105 you'll find the 12% spreadsheet and on pages 106-107 you'll find the 3% spreadsheet.

Once again, the leases are identical, all that has changed is the discount rate and therefore the discount factors in column C.

When cash flows are discounted at 12% p.a. their value reduces much faster than when they are discounted by 3% p.a. That doesn't make much of a difference in the early months. Discounting the £229.34 rental in month 2 (cell H104) reduces its value to £227.02 in the 12% p.a. evaluation and £228.77 (cell I104) in the 3% p.a. evaluation. The difference is negligible.

But now look at month 22 (cell I124). At a 12% p.a. discount rate this has a PV of £186.10 but in the 3% p.a. spreadsheet the PV is £217.63. That's a massive difference that gets even more pronounced as we get into the last year of the lease.

If you decide to buy a car, once you have laid out the initial purchase price you have to wait until you receive the two major benefits: capital allowances and sale proceeds. So most of the major cashflows are coming inwards, towards the company.

However under a lease all of the major cashflows are lease rentals and these are going outwards, away from the company.

If you buy a car and have a lower discount rate, this tends to benefit you because the future major cash flows – which are mainly inflows – have a higher present value (i.e. they aren't being discounted as much).

The reverse applies with a lease. As discount rates decline this *increases* the overall cost to the company. The major future cash flows are outflows so a lower discount rate means that these outflows cost you more because they are not being discounted by very much: you are experiencing the full pain of these outflows.

So, looking again at our summary chart above, we can now see what has happened.

As we reduced the discount rate from 12% to 3% p.a. the purchase option became more attractive. The initial £10,000 purchase price was the same under both options, so the lower discount rate only affected the future cash flows – which were mainly inflows – and which therefore increased the benefit of those inflows.

Looking next at the leases, we can see that the reduced discount rate had the opposite effect. As the discount rate declined, the future cash flows – which were mainly outflows – received the benefit of a lower discount and therefore they cost the company more in PV terms.

Hence with a lower discount rate we ended up with a different result. It was better to buy the low-CO_2 car and it cost roughly the same if you chose to buy or lease the other two cars. That was a *big* turnaround from the previous situation.

	A	B	C	D	E	F
101	1.00%	Monthly interest rate		Common to both leases		
102						
103	Month	Date	Discount factors	Rental paid	VAT paid on rental	VAT recovered on rental
103	1	01/12/2011	1.00000000	−£191.12	−£38.22	
104	2	01/01/2012	0.99009901	−£191.12	−£38.22	
105	3	01/02/2012	0.98029605	−£191.12	−£38.22	£19.11
106	4	01/03/2012	0.97059015	−£191.12	−£38.22	
107	5	01/04/2012	0.96098034	−£191.12	−£38.22	
108	6	01/05/2012	0.95146569	−£191.12	−£38.22	£57.34
109	7	01/06/2012	0.94204524	−£191.12	−£38.22	
110	8	01/07/2012	0.93271805	−£191.12	−£38.22	
111	9	01/08/2012	0.92348322	−£191.12	−£38.22	£57.34
112	10	01/09/2012	0.91433982	−£191.12	−£38.22	
113	11	01/10/2012	0.90528695	−£191.12	−£38.22	
114	12	01/11/2012	0.89632372	−£191.12	−£38.22	£57.34
115	13	01/12/2012	0.88744923	−£191.12	−£38.22	
116	14	01/01/2013	0.87866260	−£191.12	−£38.22	
117	15	01/02/2013	0.86996297	−£191.12	−£38.22	£57.34
118	16	01/03/2013	0.86134947	−£191.12	−£38.22	
119	17	01/04/2013	0.85282126	−£191.12	−£38.22	
120	18	01/05/2013	0.84437749	−£191.12	−£38.22	£57.34
121	19	01/06/2013	0.83601731	−£191.12	−£38.22	
122	20	01/07/2013	0.82773992	−£191.12	−£38.22	
123	21	01/08/2013	0.81954447	−£191.12	−£38.22	£57.34
124	22	01/09/2013	0.81143017	−£191.12	−£38.22	
125	23	01/10/2013	0.80339621	−£191.12	−£38.22	
126	24	01/11/2013	0.79544179	−£191.12	−£38.22	£57.34
127	25	01/12/2013	0.78756613	−£191.12	−£38.22	
128	26	01/01/2014	0.77976844	−£191.12	−£38.22	
129	27	01/02/2014	0.77204796	−£191.12	−£38.22	£57.34
130	28	01/03/2014	0.76440392	−£191.12	−£38.22	
131	29	01/04/2014	0.75683557	−£191.12	−£38.22	
132	30	01/05/2014	0.74934215	−£191.12	−£38.22	£57.34
133	31	01/06/2014	0.74192292	−£191.12	−£38.22	
134	32	01/07/2014	0.73457715	−£191.12	−£38.22	
135	33	01/08/2014	0.72730411	−£191.12	−£38.22	£57.34
136	34	01/09/2014	0.72010307	−£191.12	−£38.22	
137	35	01/10/2014	0.71297334	−£191.12	−£38.22	
138	36	01/11/2014	0.70591420	−£191.12	−£38.22	£57.34
139	37	01/12/2014	0.69892495			
140	38	01/01/2015	0.69200490			
141	39	01/02/2015	0.68515337			£38.22
142	40	01/03/2015	0.67836967			
143	41	01/04/2015	0.67165314			
144	42	01/05/2015	0.66500311			£0.00
145	43	01/06/2015	0.65841892			
146	44	01/07/2015	0.65189992			
147	45	01/08/2015	0.64544546			£0.00
148	46	01/09/2015	0.63905492			
149	47	01/10/2015	0.63272764			
150				−£6,880.32	−£1,376.06	£688.03
151						
152	Difference					

G	H	I	J	K	L
Leases where 100% of rental is tax deductible			Lease where 85% of rental is tax deductible		
Corp tax relief on lease rental and disallowed VAT	Net cash flows	PV	Corp tax relief on lease rental and disallowed VAT	Net cash flows	PV
	-£229.34	-£229.34		-£229.34	-£229.34
	-£229.34	-£227.07		-£229.34	-£227.07
	-£210.23	-£206.09		-£210.23	-£206.09
	-£229.34	-£222.60		-£229.34	-£222.60
	-£229.34	-£220.40		-£229.34	-£220.40
	-£172.01	-£163.66		-£172.01	-£163.66
	-£229.34	-£216.05		-£229.34	-£216.05
	-£229.34	-£213.91		-£229.34	-£213.91
	-£172.01	-£158.85		-£172.01	-£158.85
	-£229.34	-£209.70		-£229.34	-£209.70
£54.66	-£174.68	-£158.14	£46.46	-£182.88	-£165.56
	-£172.01	-£154.17		-£172.01	-£154.17
	-£229.34	-£203.53		-£229.34	-£203.53
	-£229.34	-£201.52		-£229.34	-£201.52
	-£172.01	-£149.64		-£172.01	-£149.64
	-£229.34	-£197.55		-£229.34	-£197.55
	-£229.34	-£195.59		-£229.34	-£195.59
	-£172.01	-£145.24		-£172.01	-£145.24
	-£229.34	-£191.74		-£229.34	-£191.74
	-£229.34	-£189.84		-£229.34	-£189.84
	-£172.01	-£140.97		-£172.01	-£140.97
	-£229.34	-£186.10		-£229.34	-£186.10
£651.33	£421.99	£339.02	£553.63	£324.29	£260.53
	-£172.01	-£136.82		-£172.01	-£136.82
	-£229.34	-£180.62		-£229.34	-£180.62
	-£229.34	-£178.84		-£229.34	-£178.84
	-£172.01	-£132.80		-£172.01	-£132.80
	-£229.34	-£175.31		-£229.34	-£175.31
	-£229.34	-£173.58		-£229.34	-£173.58
	-£172.01	-£128.89		-£172.01	-£128.89
	-£229.34	-£170.16		-£229.34	-£170.16
	-£229.34	-£168.47		-£229.34	-£168.47
	-£172.01	-£125.10		-£172.01	-£125.10
	-£229.34	-£165.15		-£229.34	-£165.15
£625.28	£395.93	£282.29	£531.49	£302.14	£215.42
	-£172.01	-£121.42		-£172.01	-£121.42
	£0.00	£0.00		£0.00	£0.00
	£0.00	£0.00		£0.00	£0.00
	£38.22	£26.19		£38.22	£26.19
	£0.00	£0.00		£0.00	£0.00
	£0.00	£0.00		£0.00	£0.00
	£0.00	£0.00		£0.00	£0.00
	£0.00	£0.00		£0.00	£0.00
	£0.00	£0.00		£0.00	£0.00
	£0.00	£0.00		£0.00	£0.00
	£0.00	£0.00		£0.00	£0.00
£549.28	£549.28	£347.55	£466.89	£466.89	£295.41
£1,880.55	-£5,687.80		£1,598.47	-£5,969.88	
		-£5,043.80			-£5,248.72
					-£204.92

	A	B	C	D	E	F
101	0.25%	Monthly interest rate		Common to both leases		
102	Month	Date	Discount factors	Rental paid	VAT paid on rental	VAT recovered on rental
103	1	01/12/2011	1.00000000	−£191.12	−£38.22	
104	2	01/01/2012	0.99750623	−£191.12	−£38.22	
105	3	01/02/2012	0.99501869	−£191.12	−£38.22	£19.11
106	4	01/03/2012	0.99253734	−£191.12	−£38.22	
107	5	01/04/2012	0.99006219	−£191.12	−£38.22	
108	6	01/05/2012	0.98759321	−£191.12	−£38.22	£57.34
109	7	01/06/2012	0.98513038	−£191.12	−£38.22	
110	8	01/07/2012	0.98267370	−£191.12	−£38.22	
111	9	01/08/2012	0.98022314	−£191.12	−£38.22	£57.34
112	10	01/09/2012	0.97777869	−£191.12	−£38.22	
113	11	01/10/2012	0.97534034	−£191.12	−£38.22	
114	12	01/11/2012	0.97290807	−£191.12	−£38.22	£57.34
115	13	01/12/2012	0.97048187	−£191.12	−£38.22	
116	14	01/01/2013	0.96806171	−£191.12	−£38.22	
117	15	01/02/2013	0.96564759	−£191.12	−£38.22	£57.34
118	16	01/03/2013	0.96323949	−£191.12	−£38.22	
119	17	01/04/2013	0.96083740	−£191.12	−£38.22	
120	18	01/05/2013	0.95844130	−£191.12	−£38.22	£57.34
121	19	01/06/2013	0.95605117	−£191.12	−£38.22	
122	20	01/07/2013	0.95366700	−£191.12	−£38.22	
123	21	01/08/2013	0.95128878	−£191.12	−£38.22	£57.34
124	22	01/09/2013	0.94891649	−£191.12	−£38.22	
125	23	01/10/2013	0.94655011	−£191.12	−£38.22	
126	24	01/11/2013	0.94418964	−£191.12	−£38.22	£57.34
127	25	01/12/2013	0.94183505	−£191.12	−£38.22	
128	26	01/01/2014	0.93948634	−£191.12	−£38.22	
129	27	01/02/2014	0.93714348	−£191.12	−£38.22	£57.34
130	28	01/03/2014	0.93480646	−£191.12	−£38.22	
131	29	01/04/2014	0.93247527	−£191.12	−£38.22	
132	30	01/05/2014	0.93014990	−£191.12	−£38.22	£57.34
133	31	01/06/2014	0.92783032	−£191.12	−£38.22	
134	32	01/07/2014	0.92551653	−£191.12	−£38.22	
135	33	01/08/2014	0.92320851	−£191.12	−£38.22	£57.34
136	34	01/09/2014	0.92090624	−£191.12	−£38.22	
137	35	01/10/2014	0.91860972	−£191.12	−£38.22	
138	36	01/11/2014	0.91631892	−£191.12	−£38.22	£57.34
139	37	01/12/2014	0.91403384			
140	38	01/01/2015	0.91175445			
141	39	01/02/2015	0.90948075			£38.22
142	40	01/03/2015	0.90721272			
143	41	01/04/2015	0.90495034			
144	42	01/05/2015	0.90269361			£0.00
145	43	01/06/2015	0.90044250			
146	44	01/07/2015	0.89819701			
147	45	01/08/2015	0.89595712			£0.00
148	46	01/09/2015	0.89372281			
149	47	01/10/2015	0.89149407			
150				−£6,880.32	−£1,376.06	£688.03
151						
152	Difference					

G	H	I	J	K	L
Leases where 100% of rental is tax deductible			Lease where 85% of rental is tax deductible		
Corp tax relief on lease rental and disallowed VAT	Net cash flows	PV	Corp tax relief on lease rental and disallowed VAT	Net cash flows	PV
	–£229.34	–£229.34		–£229.34	–£229.34
	–£229.34	–£228.77		–£229.34	–£228.77
	–£210.23	–£209.18		–£210.23	–£209.18
	–£229.34	–£227.63		–£229.34	–£227.63
	–£229.34	–£227.06		–£229.34	–£227.06
	–£172.01	–£169.87		–£172.01	–£169.87
	–£229.34	–£225.93		–£229.34	–£225.93
	–£229.34	–£225.37		–£229.34	–£225.37
	–£172.01	–£168.61		–£172.01	–£168.61
	–£229.34	–£224.25		–£229.34	–£224.25
£54.66	–£174.68	–£170.38	£46.46	–£182.88	–£178.37
	–£172.01	–£167.35		–£172.01	–£167.35
	–£229.34	–£222.57		–£229.34	–£222.57
	–£229.34	–£222.02		–£229.34	–£222.02
	–£172.01	–£166.10		–£172.01	–£166.10
	–£229.34	–£220.91		–£229.34	–£220.91
	–£229.34	–£220.36		–£229.34	–£220.36
	–£172.01	–£164.86		–£172.01	–£164.86
	–£229.34	–£219.26		–£229.34	–£219.26
	–£229.34	–£218.72		–£229.34	–£218.72
	–£172.01	–£163.63		–£172.01	–£163.63
	–£229.34	–£217.63		–£229.34	–£217.63
£651.33	£421.99	£399.43	£553.63	£324.29	£306.95
	–£172.01	–£162.41		–£172.01	–£162.41
	–£229.34	–£216.00		–£229.34	–£216.00
	–£229.34	–£215.47		–£229.34	–£215.47
	–£172.01	–£161.20		–£172.01	–£161.20
	–£229.34	–£214.39		–£229.34	–£214.39
	–£229.34	–£213.86		–£229.34	–£213.86
	–£172.01	–£159.99		–£172.01	–£159.99
	–£229.34	–£212.79		–£229.34	–£212.79
	–£229.34	–£212.26		–£229.34	–£212.26
	–£172.01	–£158.80		–£172.01	–£158.80
	–£229.34	–£211.20		–£229.34	–£211.20
£625.28	£395.93	£363.71	£531.49	£302.14	£277.55
	–£172.01	–£157.61		–£172.01	–£157.61
	£0.00	£0.00		£0.00	£0.00
	£0.00	£0.00		£0.00	£0.00
	£38.22	£34.76		£38.22	£34.76
	£0.00	£0.00		£0.00	£0.00
	£0.00	£0.00		£0.00	£0.00
	£0.00	£0.00		£0.00	£0.00
	£0.00	£0.00		£0.00	£0.00
	£0.00	£0.00		£0.00	£0.00
	£0.00	£0.00		£0.00	£0.00
	£0.00	£0.00		£0.00	£0.00
£549.28	£549.28	£489.68	£466.89	£466.89	£416.23
£1,880.55	–£5,687.80		£1,598.47	–£5,969.88	
		–£5,518.22			–£5,778.31
					–£260.08

You can't normally tell whether which is better, leasing or buying, just by doing mental arithmetic. Indeed, mental arithmetic will often deliver the wrong result. Only by doing a full DCF analysis and bringing in all of the relevant factors will you arrive at the real cost.

And as we have seen above it is important to choose the right discount rate.

15

EARLY TERMINATING YOUR CONTRACT HIRE AGREEMENT

IN THIS CHAPTER...

■ Early termination maths

■ The percentage of future rentals method

■ Actual cost method

■ Sliding scale according to the timing of the early termination

We have been looking at the maths you need to consider when deciding whether to lease or buy a vehicle. Now we will look at the maths involved in early terminating your contract hire agreement. Later we will look at the somewhat more complex maths involved in terminating hire purchase and similar agreements.

There are a number of reasons you may have to terminate your contract hire agreement before the contracted end-date; for example if the vehicle has been written-off in an accident or stolen, or if the driver has left your employment.

The supplier entered into the lease expecting that you would keep the vehicle until the contractual end-date. They calculated the rentals and arranged their own funding on this basis and expected to get capital allowances for the full term of the lease.

On early termination they have to:

■ clear their books

■ recover any extra costs to be borne in keeping their own funding in place until the end of the lease

■ recover any adverse effects of disrupting their capital allowance flows and (perhaps)

■ recover some element of the profit they had hoped to make had the contract run to maturity.

Many contract hire agreements are silent on what happens in the event of an early termination. This can lead to misunderstandings and disputes so it is far better to agree this in writing with the contract hire company from the outset.

There are several ways to calculate a contract hire early termination settlement figure. They include:

■ the *percentage of future rentals* method

- the *actual cost* method and

- the *sliding scale according to the timing of the early termination* method.

THE PERCENTAGE OF FUTURE RENTALS METHOD

This may be set out in your contract as a simple formula that says something like:

"If you terminate in the first 12 months we will charge you 60% of all future rentals.

"If you terminate in the second 12 months we will charge you 50% of all future rentals and

"If you terminate thereafter we will charge you 40% of all future rentals."

A different lessor might simply charge 50% of all future rentals. In fact there is no consistent way of setting this figure in the market and each supplier has their own way of calculating this charge.

When entering into the lease the supplier has no idea whether you might ask to early terminate the agreement, when this might occur, how much the vehicle would then be worth and how much any insurance settlement will be. Hence the 'percentage of outstanding rentals' settlement method is risky for the supplier and can cause them to make a loss.

Nonetheless, many contract hire companies offer this arrangement as it offers you certainty and removes the need for discussion, debate and possible disagreement at a later date.

ACTUAL COST METHOD

Under this method, the lessor:

- takes the balance outstanding in its books
- adds any arrears of rental
- adds any costs or fees it incurred to recover or sell the vehicle
- deducts the vehicle sale proceeds (or insurance payout) and
- charges you the difference.

Normally, for the sake of simplicity, capital allowance or other tax matters are ignored, though in fact these do have an impact on the profit or loss that the lessor will make on the early termination.

The actual cost method is a particularly simple way to calculate an early termination settlement and is often a feature of 'open-book' contract hire arrangements. It may also be the cheapest method of early termination available to you. For this reason it is usually only offered to large, creditworthy businesses with large fleets, where there is strong competitive pressure and the contract hire company is keen to preserve the relationship.

SLIDING SCALE ACCORDING TO THE TIMING OF THE EARLY TERMINATION

This is a refinement of the percentage of outstanding rentals method.

At the start of the agreement the supplier will provide you with a chart showing the amount that will be payable, month by month, in the event of early termination.

Here is example.

This schedule for a 36 month lease assumes a £12,000 capital cost and a £4,000 residual value. The 'rental profile' is 3+33, which means that the equivalent of three months' rental is paid on day one and that this is followed by 33 further monthly rentals, commencing one month after the start of the agreement (see table opposite).

Note that you don't have to pay anything if you terminate during months 34, 35 or 36, as no rentals are due in those months.

Whatever early termination method is used, the amount you are charged will include any arrears, interest on arrears, costs, fees or expenses that the supplier incurs in recovering and selling the vehicle.

Whilst it may be your policy to take all vehicles on lease for, say, three years, there may well be occasions when you know in advance that you are likely to need a particular vehicle for a shorter period. For example, you may need it for an overseas visitor who will be in the UK for a fixed period or for someone who plans to retire in 18 months.

In these situations you will usually save money if you enter into the lease for the shorter period at the outset. If it's likely you will need to extend the lease later it's a good idea to speak to your leasing company before signing the agreement to discuss whether and on what terms they will be prepared to extend it. While the rentals that you pay will be more expensive initially, entering a shorter lease from the outset will normally work out cheaper than signing a three-year lease and early terminating after 18 months.

Termination during month number	Amount payable £
1	4900.69
2	4752.19
3	4603.68
4	4455.17
5	4306.67
6	4158.16
7	4009.66
8	3861.15
9	3712.65
10	3564.14
11	3415.63
12	3267.13
13	2494.90
14	2376.09
15	2257.29
16	2138.48
17	2019.68
18	1900.87
19	1782.07
20	1663.27
21	1544.46
22	1425.66
23	1306.85
24	1188.05
25	801.93
26	712.83
27	623.72
28	534.62
29	445.52
30	356.41
31	267.31
32	178.21
33	89.10
34	Nil
35	Nil
36	Nil

Rather than terminate a lease early when the driver leaves your employment, try to reallocate the vehicle internally. This is normally cheaper than handing it back and paying an early settlement charge.

If you expect to have a high incidence of early termination, perhaps because you are in an industry with high staff turnover, consider taking ex-lease or used cars for some staff to avoid early termination costs.

Another option would be to lease your cars for short periods. A number of leasing companies and specialist suppliers will offer you a 'flexi-lease' for anything between 3 and 12 months.

Alternatively you could use pool cars.

16

EARLY TERMINATING YOUR FINANCE AGREEMENT

In the last chapter we looked at the main ways in which contract hire early termination figures are calculated:

■ percentage of future rentals

■ sliding scale based on time of the early termination and

■ actual cost

Now we will look at the main methods used to calculate early termination figures for hire purchase, finance lease and other agreements:

■ the annuity method and

■ the 'sum of the digits' method

When settling a hire purchase or finance lease agreement, the settlement figure must be sufficient to fully repay the lessor's/lender's investment, whereas with contract hire the supplier also has to sell the car to fully recover their investment.

THE ANNUITY METHOD

Most people know how a repayment mortgage works. You borrow a sum of money over a long period and make monthly repayments. These repayments only change if market interest rates change. By the end of the contract the mortgage has been fully repaid.

At the end of the first year when the mortgage statement arrives you may be horrified to see that, of the thousands of pounds you paid during the year, most went to repay interest and this left only a tiny amount to repay the capital borrowed.

The lender provides the reassuring explanation:

"Don't worry, we have not made a mistake, this is perfectly normal, you owe more in the early years so most of the repayment is interest but in later years this will reverse and most of your repayment will be capital."

The same principle works with any hire purchase agreement, conditional sale, contract purchase or finance lease agreement. In the early months the repayments are mainly interest, in the later months mainly capital.

Here is an example:

A vehicle costs £10,000. The 3-year hire purchase agreement calls for thirty-six equal monthly repayments, each payable at the start of the month, the first being made when the vehicle is delivered. The interest rate is 12% per annum nominal, which equates to 1% per month. The repayments are £328.85 per month. (See table on page 120.)

This calculation (which was produced using the Goal Seek function in Excel), is called an annuity or an actuarial calculation. Note how the interest amount is higher in early months, lower in later months.

The fact that the repayments are split between interest and capital is an economic fact of life and occurs regardless of the way the funder chooses to record the loan or lease in their books.

On early termination there will usually be a balance outstanding in the funder's books that exceeds the then-current value of the vehicle being financed. The only exceptions are where you have paid a large initial deposit, or the vehicle has retained its value remarkably well, or a combination of the two.

Therefore the amount the funder needs to charge you simply to break even on an early termination may come as a surprise to you.

	Opening balance £	Payment £	Interest £	Capital £	Closing balance £
1	10000.00	328.85	96.71	232.14	9767.86
2	9767.86	328.85	94.39	234.46	9533.39
3	9533.39	328.85	92.05	236.81	9296.58
4	9296.58	328.85	89.68	239.18	9057.41
5	9057.41	328.85	87.29	241.57	8815.84
6	8815.84	328.85	84.87	243.98	8571.85
7	8571.85	328.85	82.43	246.42	8325.43
8	8325.43	328.85	79.97	248.89	8076.54
9	8076.54	328.85	77.48	251.38	7825.16
10	7825.16	328.85	74.96	253.89	7571.27
11	7571.27	328.85	72.42	256.43	7314.84
12	7314.84	328.85	69.86	258.99	7055.84
13	7055.84	328.85	67.27	261.58	6794.26
14	6794.26	328.85	64.65	264.20	6530.06
15	6530.06	328.85	62.01	266.84	6263.22
16	6263.22	328.85	59.34	269.51	5993.71
17	5993.71	328.85	56.65	272.21	5721.50
18	5721.50	328.85	53.93	274.93	5446.57
19	5446.57	328.85	51.18	277.68	5168.89
20	5168.89	328.85	48.40	280.45	4888.44
21	4888.44	328.85	45.60	283.26	4605.18
22	4605.18	328.85	42.76	286.09	4319.09
23	4319.09	328.85	39.90	288.95	4030.14
24	4030.14	328.85	37.01	291.84	3738.30
25	3738.30	328.85	34.09	294.76	3443.54
26	3443.54	328.85	31.15	297.71	3145.83
27	3145.83	328.85	28.17	300.68	2845.14
28	2845.14	328.85	25.16	303.69	2541.45
29	2541.45	328.85	22.13	306.73	2234.72
30	2234.72	328.85	19.06	309.80	1924.93
31	1924.93	328.85	15.96	312.89	1612.03
32	1612.03	328.85	12.83	316.02	1296.01
33	1296.01	328.85	9.67	319.18	976.83
34	976.83	328.85	6.48	322.37	654.45
35	654.45	328.85	3.26	325.60	328.85
36	328.85	328.85	0.00	328.85	0.00

THE SUM OF THE DIGITS METHOD

Clearly, it would be helpful if the borrower had a simple method to help them calculate how much interest was due each month. If they could work this out they would be able to calculate the proportion of each payment that goes to reduce the capital balance each month and therefore the outstanding balance they have to pay on early termination.

You can't work out annuity balances using mental arithmetic and most people don't have financial calculators. Therefore a simplified calculation method was required and the one that was developed is called the 'sum of the digits method' (it is also called the Rule of 78). It works as a good substitute for the more complex (but more accurate) actuarial calculation.

Under the sum of the digits method, rather than charging interest on the balance outstanding each month, the whole interest charge for the contract is spread across the life of the agreement using a weighting system.

Once again, it's best to illustrate this with an example and we will use the same facts as before.

The client borrowed £10,000 and has to repay £328.85 x 36, that is, a total of £11,838.76. Therefore the interest they are paying totals £1,838.76.

Now we will do something strange and add up 1 + 2 + 3 + 4 and so on up to 36. The sum of numbers 1 to 36 is 666. (Which some may find a little spooky).

The first payment repays £99.39 of interest under the Rule of 78. That's calculated as 36 ÷ 666 x £1,838.76.

The second payment repays slightly less: 35 ÷ 666 x £1,838.76, that is, £96.36.

The full schedule for this example is shown on the next page.

Payment No.	Rule of 78 Calculation	£
1	36 ÷ 666 x £1,838.76 =	99.39
2	35 ÷ 666 x £1,838.76 =	96.63
3	34 ÷ 666 x £1,838.76 =	93.87
4	33 ÷ 666 x £1,838.76 =	91.11
5	32 ÷ 666 x £1,838.76 =	88.35
6	31 ÷ 666 x £1,838.76 =	85.59
7	30 ÷ 666 x £1,838.76 =	82.83
8	29 ÷ 666 x £1,838.76 =	80.07
9	28 ÷ 666 x £1,838.76 =	77.31
10	27 ÷ 666 x £1,838.76 =	74.54
11	26 ÷ 666 x £1,838.76 =	71.78
12	25 ÷ 666 x £1,838.76 =	69.02
13	24 ÷ 666 x £1,838.76 =	66.26
14	23 ÷ 666 x £1,838.76 =	63.50
15	22 ÷ 666 x £1,838.76 =	60.74
16	21 ÷ 666 x £1,838.76 =	57.98
17	20 ÷ 666 x £1,838.76 =	55.22
18	19 ÷ 666 x £1,838.76 =	52.46
19	18 ÷ 666 x £1,838.76 =	49.70
20	17 ÷ 666 x £1,838.76 =	46.94
21	16 ÷ 666 x £1,838.76 =	44.17
22	15 ÷ 666 x £1,838.76 =	41.41
23	14 ÷ 666 x £1,838.76 =	38.65
24	13 ÷ 666 x £1,838.76 =	35.89
25	12 ÷ 666 x £1,838.76 =	33.13
26	11 ÷ 666 x £1,838.76 =	30.37
27	10 ÷ 666 x £1,838.76 =	27.61
28	9 ÷ 666 x £1,838.76 =	24.85
29	8 ÷ 666 x £1,838.76 =	22.09
30	7 ÷ 666 x £1,838.76 =	19.33
31	6 ÷ 666 x £1,838.76 =	16.57
32	5 ÷ 666 x £1,838.76 =	13.80
33	4 ÷ 666 x £1,838.76 =	11.04
34	3 ÷ 666 x £1,838.76 =	8.28
35	2 ÷ 666 x £1,838.76 =	5.52
36	1 ÷ 666 x £1,838.76 =	2.76

If you compare the actuarial calculation with the Rule of 78 calculation you will note that the latter gives us a pretty close approximation of the more accurate actuarial figures.

The difference is shown on this chart:

Payment No.	Actuarial	Rule of 78	Difference
	£	£	£
1	96.71	99.39	2.68
2	94.39	96.63	2.24
3	92.05	93.87	1.83
4	89.68	91.11	1.43
5	87.29	88.35	1.06
6	84.87	85.59	0.72
7	82.43	82.83	0.40
8	79.97	80.07	0.10
9	77.48	77.31	-0.17
10	74.96	74.54	-0.42
11	72.42	71.78	-0.64
12	69.86	69.02	-0.84
13	67.27	66.26	-1.01
14	64.65	63.50	-1.15
15	62.01	60.74	-1.27
16	59.34	57.98	-1.36
17	56.65	55.22	-1.43
18	53.93	52.46	-1.47
19	51.18	49.70	-1.48
20	48.40	46.94	-1.47
21	45.60	44.17	-1.42
22	42.76	41.41	-1.35
23	39.90	38.65	-1.25
24	37.01	35.89	-1.12
25	34.09	33.13	-0.96
26	31.15	30.37	-0.78
27	28.17	27.61	-0.56
28	25.16	24.85	-0.31
29	22.13	22.09	-0.04
			continued

30	19.06	19.33	0.27
31	15.96	16.57	0.60
32	12.83	13.80	0.97
33	9.67	11.04	1.37
34	6.48	8.28	1.80
35	3.26	5.52	2.27
36	0.00	2.76	2.76

To determine a Rule of 78 early termination figure, we use the Rule of 78 interest figures to replace the balances shown in the first chart, thus:

Payment No.	Opening balance £	Payment £	Rule of 78 Interest £	Capital Repayment £	Closing balance £
1	10000.00	328.85	99.39	229.46	9770.54
2	9770.54	328.85	96.63	232.22	9538.31
3	9538.31	328.85	93.87	234.98	9303.33
4	9303.33	328.85	91.11	237.74	9065.59
5	9065.59	328.85	88.35	240.51	8825.08
6	8825.08	328.85	85.59	243.27	8581.81
7	8581.81	328.85	82.83	246.03	8335.79
8	8335.79	328.85	80.07	248.79	8087.00
9	8087.00	328.85	77.31	251.55	7835.45
10	7835.45	328.85	74.54	254.31	7581.14
11	7581.14	328.85	71.78	257.07	7324.07
12	7324.07	328.85	69.02	259.83	7064.24
13	7064.24	328.85	66.26	262.59	6801.64
14	6801.64	328.85	63.50	265.35	6536.29
15	6536.29	328.85	60.74	268.11	6268.17
16	6268.17	328.85	57.98	270.88	5997.30
17	5997.30	328.85	55.22	273.64	5723.66
18	5723.66	328.85	52.46	276.40	5447.26
19	5447.26	328.85	49.70	279.16	5168.11
20	5168.11	328.85	46.94	281.92	4886.19
21	4886.19	328.85	44.17	284.68	4601.51
22	4601.51	328.85	41.41	287.44	4314.07
23	4314.07	328.85	38.65	290.20	4023.86
24	4023.86	328.85	35.89	292.96	3730.90
25	3730.90	328.85	33.13	295.72	3435.18
26	3435.18	328.85	30.37	298.48	3136.69
27	3136.69	328.85	27.61	301.25	2835.45
28	2835.45	328.85	24.85	304.01	2531.44
29	2531.44	328.85	22.09	306.77	2224.67
30	2224.67	328.85	19.33	309.53	1915.14
31	1915.14	328.85	16.57	312.29	1602.86
32	1602.86	328.85	13.80	315.05	1287.81
33	1287.81	328.85	11.04	317.81	969.99
34	969.99	328.85	8.28	320.57	649.42
35	649.42	328.85	5.52	323.33	326.09
36	326.09	328.85	2.76	326.09	0.00

So under Rule of 78, the balances at the end of each month are pretty similar to those calculated using the actuarial method.

The Rule of 78 gets its name from the fact that it represents the sum of the numbers from 1 to 12. So, in calculating a Rule of 78 settlement in a one-year contract, the denominator in the formula would be 78, not 666. (I believe the expression 'Rule of 78' was first coined in the 1930s when 1-year hire purchase agreements were the norm).

Your actual contract may say that 1, 2 or more months' interest must be added to the Rule of 78 figure when calculating the actual settlement amount.

If you decide to hand back the vehicle (and if the lessor agrees to take it back and sell it), these early termination settlement amounts will be reduced by the actual or projected sale proceeds of the vehicle.

17

IT'S NOT ALL
1+35

IN THIS CHAPTER...

■ Rental patterns, residual values and balloon rentals

■ Regular initial rental, high initial rental, spread rental and all in advance

■ The effect of residual values and balloon rentals on rental calculations

■ The difference between contract hire and HP quotes

In this chapter we are going to have a look at rental patterns, residual values and balloon rentals.

When you ask a leasing company for a quote they will ask you which rental pattern (or 'payment profile') you require.

There are four patterns:

- regular initial rental
- high initial rental
- spread rental
- all in advance

With a **regular initial rental** you will pay the same amount on day 1 as you pay monthly throughout the contract. Typical profiles are 1+35 or 1+47.

This profile is normally offered to public sector bodies and large companies, where the lessor doesn't need to take any extra payment up front as a cushion against client default.

If you opt for a **high initial rental** you will pay 3 or sometimes 6 rentals on delivery. A typical 3-year payment profile is 3+33. You pay two extra rentals on delivery so you don't need to pay any rentals at the start of months 35 and 36. Four-year business is often transacted with a 3+45 payment profile.

This profile is usually offered to private individuals, smaller fleets and SMEs.

Rather than lease your car by paying monthly rentals on a 3+33 or 1+35 basis, you might instead opt to pay a high initial payment (the initial 3) followed by 35 monthly payments, i.e. 3+35. The rentals will be lower than would have been paid under a 3+33 arrangement but you will have to pay more of them. This profile is called a **spread rental**, presumably because it spreads the rentals over another two months.

It is common for lease brokers to offer spread rentals.

Some hirers ask to pay **all payments in advance**. This would make no sense at all on a hire purchase agreement. If you can afford to buy the vehicle there is no reason to set up a finance agreement.

However, on contract hire agreements it is not unusual for cash-rich companies to request this. They do so to take advantage of the lessor's ability to recover input VAT when buying the vehicle. The lessor ends up just funding the residual value so that the client bears little interest cost.

Contract hire is an operating lease – a simple rental agreement – so there is no particular reason why rentals should not be paid in advance if both parties agree. After all, if an equipment hire shop can ask for payment in advance when you hire a piece of equipment, why not pre-pay to hire a car for a few years if you have the cash?

RESIDUAL VALUES AND BALLOON RENTALS

Next we need to look at the effect that residual values and balloon rentals have on rental calculations.

If a lender builds a residual value or balloon rental into your finance agreement they will be able to reduce your regular monthly payments and still earn the return they require.

In the cash flow on the next page, the lender finances a £14,000 vehicle over twenty-four months.

Payments are monthly in arrears. The nominal interest rate is 12% p.a. or 1% per month.

Month	Opening balance £	Interest £	Payment £	Closing balance £
1	14000.00	140.00	659.03	13480.97
2	13480.97	134.81	659.03	12956.75
3	12956.75	129.57	659.03	12427.29
4	12427.29	124.27	659.03	11892.54
5	11892.54	118.93	659.03	11352.43
6	11352.43	113.52	659.03	10806.93
7	10806.93	108.07	659.03	10255.97
8	10255.97	102.56	659.03	9699.50
9	9699.50	96.99	659.03	9137.47
10	9137.47	91.37	659.03	8569.81
11	8569.81	85.70	659.03	7996.48
12	7996.48	79.96	659.03	7417.42
13	7417.42	74.17	659.03	6832.56
14	6832.56	68.33	659.03	6241.86
15	6241.86	62.42	659.03	5645.25
16	5645.25	56.45	659.03	5042.67
17	5042.67	50.43	659.03	4434.07
18	4434.07	44.34	659.03	3819.38
19	3819.38	38.19	659.03	3198.55
20	3198.55	31.99	659.03	2571.51
21	2571.51	25.72	659.03	1938.19
22	1938.19	19.38	659.03	1298.55
23	1298.55	12.99	659.03	652.50
24	652.50	6.53	659.03	0.00

Note how the equal monthly repayments of £659.03 reduce the balance outstanding in the lender's books to zero once the final payment has been made.

This could be the cash flow for a conditional sale agreement in which you are being asked to pay £659.03 for twenty-four months. After making the final payment you would become the owner of the vehicle.

Let us now assume instead that you decide to fund the vehicle using contract hire. When you hand it back at the end of the agreement the lessor has to sell it to recover the balance of their investment. In this example they believe the car will be worth £8,000 on disposal, so they build this amount into the rental calculation.

The cash flow now looks like this:

Month	Opening balance £	Interest £	Payment £	Closing balance £
1	14000.00	140.00	362.44	13777.56
2	13777.56	137.78	362.44	13552.89
3	13552.89	135.53	362.44	13325.98
4	13325.98	133.26	362.44	13096.80
5	13096.80	130.97	362.44	12865.33
6	12865.33	128.65	362.44	12631.54
7	12631.54	126.32	362.44	12395.42
8	12395.42	123.95	362.44	12156.93
9	12156.93	121.57	362.44	11916.06
10	11916.06	119.16	362.44	11672.78
11	11672.78	116.73	362.44	11427.06
12	11427.06	114.27	362.44	11178.89
13	11178.89	111.79	362.44	10928.24
14	10928.24	109.28	362.44	10675.08
15	10675.08	106.75	362.44	10419.39
16	10419.39	104.19	362.44	10161.15
17	10161.15	101.61	362.44	9900.32
18	9900.32	99.00	362.44	9636.88
19	9636.88	96.37	362.44	9370.81
20	9370.81	93.71	362.44	9102.07
21	9102.07	91.02	362.44	8830.65
22	8830.65	88.31	362.44	8556.52
23	8556.52	85.57	362.44	8279.64
24	8279.64	82.80	362.44	8000.00

The lessor only needs to receive a rental of £362.44 to recover their capital investment and interest on this transaction. Note how the interest rate is still 12% p.a. nominal, or 1% per month. They are charging a smaller rental whilst still making the return they require.

The rental will be lower still if the lessor believes that the car will sell for more than £8,000, or higher if they believe it will sell for less.

If you take a car on contract hire, the lessor takes residual value risk. You can compare quotes from different suppliers and choose the cheapest quote. You don't need to be concerned with the estimated residual value that each lessor included in its calculations.

However if you get contract hire and HP quotes on the same car you need to be mindful of the differences between these two transactions.

In the HP transaction, you will be taking the residual value risk and the funder may offer you low rentals followed by a high balloon payment that you are obliged to pay.

There is a limit to the amount that a lender can stretch this in order to offer you a low-sounding monthly payment. If he makes it too low and leaves you having to pay a large balloon payment, he runs the risk that you may be unable to make this payment and the further risk that if he repossesses the car it may not fetch this amount on resale.

Continuing the above example, let us imagine that several contract hire companies quoted you rentals at around £251.22 per month for a particular car on non-maintenance contract hire. A finance company suggests that you take the same car on HP at £214.55 per month.

Here is the cash flow for the HP deal, showing that you will have to make a balloon payment of £12,000.

Month	Opening balance £	Interest £	Payment £	Closing balance £
1	14000.00	140.00	214.15	13925.85
2	13925.85	139.26	214.15	13850.96
3	13850.96	138.51	214.15	13775.33
4	13775.33	137.75	214.15	13698.93
5	13698.93	136.99	214.15	13621.78
6	13621.78	136.22	214.15	13543.85
7	13543.85	135.44	214.15	13465.14
8	13465.14	134.65	214.15	13385.64
9	13385.64	133.86	214.15	13305.35
10	13305.35	133.05	214.15	13224.26
11	13224.26	132.24	214.15	13142.35
12	13142.35	131.42	214.15	13059.63
13	13059.63	130.60	214.15	12976.08
14	12976.08	129.76	214.15	12891.69
15	12891.69	128.92	214.15	12806.46
16	12806.46	128.06	214.15	12720.38
17	12720.38	127.20	214.15	12633.44
18	12633.44	126.33	214.15	12545.63
19	12545.63	125.46	214.15	12456.94
20	12456.94	124.57	214.15	12367.36
21	12367.36	123.67	214.15	12276.88
22	12276.88	122.77	214.15	12185.51
23	12185.51	121.86	214.15	12093.21
24	12093.21	120.93	214.15	12000.00

From the earlier cash flow you can deduce that the contract hire companies believe the car will be worth £11,000 at the end of the contract. The monthly cost under the HP deal might be lower, but if you opt for HP and the contract hire companies are right, you might well be out of pocket by £1,000 when you sell the car in 3 years' time.

18

MORE ABOUT
INTEREST RATES

We have already looked at these different types of interest rate:

■ Simple

■ Flat

■ Compound

■ Nominal

■ True

■ Annual Percentage Rate (APR).

Those names are just *labels* – different ways of *describing* interest rates.

So if you are being charged £1,000 interest for borrowing £15,000 over three years, that £1,000 might be described as:

■ A% simple interest or

■ B% flat rate interest or

■ C% compound interest or

■ D% APR

Those labels don't tell you how the lender will calculate the actual amount of interest they are going to charge you, so that's the topic we're going to look at in this chapter.

In most UK leases and hire purchase agreements, your payments remain static regardless of changes in market interest rates. So they are '**fixed rate**' transactions.

If on the other hand you have funded your cars by using, say, your bank overdraft – where the interest charge varies with market interest rates (in this case bank base rates) – you will have funded them at **variable rate** or floating rate.

Most financial products, including hire purchase and leases, can be offered at fixed or variable rates.

With a fixed rate deal you know how much you must pay over the contract period, so you have no 'interest rate risk'. If market interest rates rise you still pay the same amount. Then again, if they fall you don't get any benefit.

Choose a variable rate contract instead and you take the full market interest rate risk, though you may be happy to do this if you think market interest rates are likely to fall.

Fixed rate contracts are easy to administer and they make planning simple. With variable rates you'll never be sure how much you have to pay and you will have to check every charge because it may well differ from the previous one.

Before deciding whether to go for a fixed or variable deal, consider the replacement pattern of your fleet. If most of your vehicles are due to be replaced soon and you think interest rates are likely to fall in future, it makes sense to opt for a variable rate deal.

However, if your replacements will be spread fairly evenly over the next few years and you opt for fixed rate contracts, the fixed rates you pay may well average out to be the same as the average of the interest rates across that period anyway, so you might as well choose a fixed rate deal and keep the admin simpler.

If you choose a variable rate deal, the amount you pay will rise or fall with market interest rates over the life of the contract. The contract will specify a benchmark to use in the variable rate calculation, perhaps bank base rate, Finance House Base Rate (FHBR) or London Interbank Offered Rate (LIBOR).

There is no one '**bank base rate**'. Every bank publishes its own base rate. Clearing banks tend to move theirs in unison but some smaller banks have higher base rates, reflecting their higher borrowing costs. So your variable rate contract will need to specify which bank's base rate is to be used.

LIBOR is the benchmark rate used by banks to borrow money from each other. If a major bank borrows from another major bank, it pays LIBOR plus a tiny margin. LIBOR moves frequently, often several times a minute, so your LIBOR-based finance agreement needs to be very specific about how and when that LIBOR rate is to be calculated. It is not unusual to see agreements referring to "LIBOR quoted at 10.00 a.m."

To add to the complexity there are different Sterling LIBOR rates for different periods, e.g. 'overnight LIBOR', 'one-month LIBOR', 'three-month LIBOR' and so on. If your finance agreement calls for the interest rate to be set and adjusted quarterly, it is likely that the three-month LIBOR rate will be used, as this will be equal to the lender's borrowing costs for that period.

Finance House Base Rate (FHBR) is the average of three-month Sterling LIBOR rates in the money market over the previous eight weeks, rounded up to the next half point. It is published monthly by the Finance & Leasing Association (FLA) and is shown on their website www.fla.org.uk

So, for example, your vehicle finance hire purchase agreement might be priced at "FHBR+3%". The agreement will be very specific about how any movements in FHBR will affect your repayments. As LIBOR is a nominal interest rate, so is FHBR.

After the LIBOR scandal of summer 2012 we may find in time that LIBOR is replaced by another benchmark. Until that happens it will remain a very important market rate, used for millions of transactions every day.

It is worthwhile considering here the difference between base rates and long term interest rates.

Bank base rates reflect short term money market considerations and can change frequently according to macro-economic pressures, e.g. changes in levels of government spending, concerns about the exchange rate, the inflation outlook, etc.

Longer term interest rates, for example one-year LIBOR, reflect what lenders and borrowers think market rates will be doing in the longer term. If they think that short term interest rates are low and are likely to rise, long term rates today will be higher than short term rates.

Over the years I've heard many business managers ask why their lease rates haven't fallen immediately after bank base rates have come down. There is a good reason for this. A leasing company offering you a fixed rate deal over three years will normally borrow this money over three years to lock-in ("fix") their cost of money over that period. The cost of 3 year money will often be quite different from the cost of short term money, which means that there is no direct relationship between bank base rates and the lessor's cost of funds. So if bank base rates rise or fall by, say, 1% there is no particular reason to expect leasing rates to rise or fall by the same amount.

If you enter into a variable rate agreement, the lender will normally calculate your payments by using either:

- the fixed capital with variable interest method or
- the fixed rentals with annual adjustment method.

I've also seen contracts where all the adjustments for interest rate movements have been done at the end of the contract, but this is rare.

If you have a **fixed capital with variable interest rate** contract, you will make a fixed monthly capital repayment throughout the contract, as well as a monthly or quarterly interest payment based on the then-current market interest rates.

Here is an example. We will ignore VAT and assume that no balloon rental applies.

> You agree to enter into a 3 year finance lease on a £36,000 vehicle at FHBR+4%. You will make thirty-six monthly

payments in advance of £1,000. In addition, at the end of every month, you will pay interest on the outstanding balance.

During the first month you owed £36,000 - £1,000 = £35,000. FHBR for that month was 2%, so FHBR + 4% equals 6% per annum, or 0.5% per month. As 0.5% x £35,000 equals £175, you pay £175 interest at the end of the first month at the same time as you make the second capital repayment of £1,000.

If you have a **fixed rentals with annual adjustment** contract, the rental will be calculated at the start of the contract, based on then-current market interest rates, and you will pay this throughout the agreement. At the end of each year, the lender will calculate an annual adjustment to bring the amount you have paid into line with the actual performance of an interest rate index during the year. This is sometimes called the 'notional' basis.

So, for example, using the details in the example above, let's assume you pay £1,150 per month for thirty-six months. If FHBR fell gradually during the year you will have paid more by the end of the year than was necessary. In the background the lessor would track the amount overpaid and at the end of the year they would repay it to you. If FHBR had risen, you would have underpaid and would be charged the difference.

As market interest rates fluctuate all the time, in some months you may owe money to the lessor and in others they may owe you money, but the annual adjustment saves admin for both parties.

Next we will look at **A & B Factors**, which will mainly be of interest to you if you work for a leasing or finance company, or if you work for a car dealer and a third party funder provides finance to help your customers buy cars from you.

Lessors usually have to borrow to fund their activities.

Large lessors, particularly bank-owned ones, get funds from their parent group and are told the cost of funds.

Smaller lessors use bank funding (back-to-back or undisclosed agency) on a deal-by-deal basis, paying the bank a monthly amount and a terminal balloon amount equal to the expected residual value of the car.

They may be financing hundreds of cars each month so it is not practical for them to ask the bank to quote the repayment required on each car. Therefore a practical problem arises: how does the lessor know how much it will cost to finance each car?

They might ask their bank funder to say how much they expect to be repaid for each £1,000 financed. However, if two cars cost the same amount and have different residual values, the bank would need different balloon payments and would therefore expect different monthly rentals. Every make and model of car has a different expected residual value, and these change over time.

The banks solve this problem by producing rate charts showing A and B factors (sometimes called Positive and Negative factors).

These are used as follows:

1 The capital cost of the car is multiplied by the A factor.

2 The residual value (or balloon rental) is multiplied by the B factor.

3 The result of step 2 is deducted from the result of step 1

4 The net result is the monthly repayment that should be made to the bank.

19

'PURCHASE-TYPE' FINANCE AGREEMENTS

IN THIS CHAPTER...

- Outright purchase
- Hire purchase
- Lease purchase
- Conditional sale
- Credit sale

Should you lease or buy? So far we have explored many of the issues you need to consider when answering this question.

And we've covered a lot of ground.

We've introduced the concept of discounted cash flow, seen how to calculate discount factors and looked at this formula,

$$PV = \sum_{1}^{36} \frac{PMT^n}{(1 + i)^n}$$

We then saw how to use Excel to calculate the monthly finance instalment (or rental) when you know an interest rate, and how to calculate the interest rate when you know the monthly instalment.

We then did some more complex NPV calculations using the rather wonderful Goal Seek feature within Excel.

Excel contains some other features that are very helpful when analysing lease calculations, so we looked at:

■ the PMT function (to calculate a lease rental),

■ the PV function (to calculate a present value) and

■ the RATE function (to calculate the interest rate).

There is a tax implication to almost every investment decision you make, so we then looked at how to bring VAT and corporation tax (or income tax for sole traders and partnerships) into a lease v buy analysis.

This took us into the tax rules that affect lease v buy decisions, the somewhat bizarre territory of capital allowances on company cars, and some pretty detailed Excel spreadsheets where we explored what happens when we change discount factors.

As we saw, discount rates really do make a difference and can swing the decision about whether you should lease or buy.

We then looked at a number of different types of interest rate

– simple interest, flat rates, compound interest, nominal rate of interest, true rate of interest and annual percentage rates (APRs) – and in the last couple of chapters we have looked at rental patterns and market interest rates.

Along the way I have mentioned a whole raft of financial products – outright purchase, contract hire, lease purchase, contract purchase, finance lease, hire purchase and so on – without stopping to explain these or to consider their advantages and disadvantages.

So that's what we will be doing in the next few chapters.

And we will start with **outright purchase**.

Despite the popularity of other methods of acquisition and particularly contract hire, outright purchase is still the favoured acquisition method for around half of business vehicles in the UK, so we need to consider this important method.

Companies buy their own vehicles for a variety of reasons. For many, this is simply the approach they have always adopted. Some are suspicious about involving a third party ('Surely it must cost more? They have to make a profit too'). Others buy their vehicles because they like the idea of 'ownership' and all that this implies, including the ability to place an asset on their balance sheets and have complete control of when they sell it. Some like the idea of keeping the full sale proceeds. And some like having a close working relationship with a local car dealer who will look after them and their vehicles should anything go wrong.

The move away from outright purchase started decades ago and was hastened by the 1995 VAT changes which allowed leasing companies to recover VAT on the purchase of new cars. This benefit was not available to most other businesses buying cars for their own use, so the net cost of leasing a car fell relative to buying outright.

In the absence of special arrangements made with a leasing or fleet management company, if you decide to buy your own cars you will be fully exposed to movements in the used vehicles market when you come to sell. In other words, you will take the residual value risk.

Unless your fleet is very large, when you buy your own cars you will not get the same levels of dealer and manufacturer discounts (called 'volume related bonuses') that leasing companies can attract. These can be significant.

Under the current lease accounting rules, when you buy a vehicle you have to show it as an asset ('capitalise it') on your company balance sheet. If yours is a private company this may be of no consequence to you. However, directors of quoted companies are keen to present their financial statements to shareholders and stock market analysts in the most favourable light possible and they worry that if they add assets to the balance sheet they will dilute their published return on assets.

However, upcoming lease accounting rule changes are likely to make many companies capitalise almost all assets on their balances sheets, regardless of how they are funded.

Outright purchase may tie up the working capital your company needs for its normal day-to-day trading activity.

Next we need to consider **hire purchase**

HP is defined in Statement of Standard Accounting Practice 21 as:

> "a contract for the hire of an asset that contains a provision giving the hirer an option to acquire legal title to the asset upon the fulfilment of certain conditions stated in the contract."

Note the use of the word 'hire'. The contract is essentially a hire agreement. You only become the owner if you opt to acquire legal title (ownership) at the end of the agreement. It is not unusual to see hire purchase described as 'lease with option to purchase'.

For most people, however, hire purchase is simply a way to buy a vehicle on deferred payment terms and for this reason the word 'buyer' is normally used to describe the client, rather than the word 'hirer', and the payments are called 'instalments' or 'payments' rather than 'rentals'.

The HP agreement will give you the option to buy the vehicle for a nominal 'bargain' amount at the end of the agreement. You could pay this to get title but only if you want to. If you prefer, you could simply pay the instalments and walk away.

Unlike conditional sale (see below), the option to buy is just that – an option – and not a contractual obligation. Normally though, you will pay the option amount and take title.

A hire purchase agreement is a financing agreement that gives you all the risks and rewards of ownership from the date of delivery, including residual value risk. Therefore, for accounting purposes the vehicle has to be shown as an asset on your company's balance sheet, together with a corresponding liability representing the balance due to the funder, much as if you had financed the vehicle using a loan or a finance lease.

In nearly all hire purchase transactions you expect to become the owner. The tax regime recognises this and treats hire purchase as a deferred purchase agreement rather than a hire agreement. Hence for corporation tax purposes the vehicle is deemed to belong to you from the date of delivery and you can claim capital allowances as if you had paid for it in full on delivery.

The lease rental tax disallowance rules don't apply to hire purchase payments.

For VAT purposes the 'supply' of the vehicle is deemed to have happened at the time of delivery. The funder charges output tax on the sale and you account for input tax on the purchase. The HP instalments are not subject to VAT, unlike rental or leasing arrangements.

HP is widely available from contract hire companies, finance companies and banks and it is suitable for borrowers who want to buy their vehicles on deferred payment terms.

The advantages of hire purchase are that:

■ it is a simple method of finance

■ you can obtain capital allowances from the date of delivery and

■ you do not suffer a partial lease rental tax disallowance (see earlier chapter on tax treatment).

The disadvantages of hire purchase are that:

■ it is an on balance sheet form of finance (a disadvantage for some) and

■ you retain the residual value risk.

A **lease purchase** agreement is exactly the same as a hire purchase agreement except that a balloon instalment is payable at the end of the contract. This reduces the monthly payment and makes it similar to the amounts payable under other finance products that incorporate either balloon payments (e.g. finance leases) or residual values (e.g. non-maintenance contract hire).

'Lease purchase' is a contradiction in terms; it is not a lease, simply a method of deferred purchase.

Generally, the expression 'hire purchase' is used in both commercial and consumer transactions, while 'lease purchase' is reserved for commercial transactions.

If the final balloon instalment has been calculated accurately and equals the market value of the vehicle at the end of the contract, the sale proceeds will cover the balloon payment so you will not be left out of pocket.

A **conditional sale agreement** allows you to buy a vehicle, subject to meeting all of the conditions of the agreement. Unlike hire purchase, with conditional sale you are contractually committed to become the owner of the vehicle once all of the payments have been made. The funder retains title until you have met all of your obligations, whereupon title automatically passes to you.

A conditional sale agreement is non-cancellable. There is no need for an 'option-to-purchase' fee to be paid, as title passes automatically when the last payment is made.

Conditional sale has all of the advantages of hire purchase. It is agreed in advance that you will complete the purchase of the vehicle. The only (minor) disadvantage is that it compels you to complete the purchase of the vehicle.

When conditional sale is used as the basis for a contract purchase agreement (which we will cover later), this disadvantage is overcome by using a separate agreement that allows the funder to take back the vehicle at the end of the contract for a pre-agreed price.

Credit sale is yet another form of finance that is very similar to hire purchase or conditional sale, except that here title passes to the customer at the start of the agreement, rather than the end. As this involves the funder giving up the security of ownership of the asset, credit sale was not a common form of finance.

However, this changed after employee car ownership schemes (ECOS) grew in popularity in the 1990s. This is because car benefit in kind tax rules don't apply if title in the vehicle transfers to the employee. Credit sale agreements are used in ECO schemes to transfer ownership in the vehicle to the employee on day one and therefore to avoid car benefit tax.

20

LEASE
PRODUCTS

Having looked at the implications of buying a vehicle, or financing it using a purchase-type method such as hire purchase or lease purchase, we now need to turn our attention to lease products.

But first we need to ask the question: what is a lease?

Leasing is not defined in legislation. It is a contract for the hiring (or bailment) of goods or equipment, bailment being a long-established legal concept under which a person agrees to part with possession of something they will recover at a future date.

There is a substantial body of law in this area, which the courts will apply in the event that the contract is silent on a particular issue.

The lease agreement will refer to the Lessee, the Client or the Hirer – the person who is granted the use of the vehicle for the period of the lease, subject to payment of rentals and meeting the other contractual obligations. It will also refer to the Lessor, the Owner, the Company, Us or We – the party granting the lease – which may be a contract hire company, bank, finance company, leasing company or a motor dealership that leases vehicles.

The lessor may not be the owner of the vehicle. It may be an intermediary (a small contract hire company) using a funder's vehicles and acting as their undisclosed agent. It's worthwhile asking who owns the vehicle because if something goes wrong with the lessor's business you may find yourself dealing with an organisation you have not heard of before.

Contract hire is the most popular method of vehicle finance in the UK. 'Contract hire' is a British vehicle leasing industry expression: in most other counties it would be called an *operating lease* or a *closed-end lease*.

Under contract hire, the supplier leases you a vehicle for a fixed period and mileage in return for a fixed rental. At the end of the lease, so long the vehicle has not been driven more than the agreed mileage and is in fair condition, you simply return it without further cost.

In calculating the rental the supplier will estimate the likely sale proceeds of the vehicle at the end of the lease (the 'residual value' or 'RV'). If the vehicle eventually sells for more or less than this, the supplier will make a profit or loss respectively. Normally, as lessee you will have no financial interest in this profit or loss.

Through this mechanism the supplier is said to take the 'residual value risk' in the vehicle.

As you don't pay the residual value, one way of viewing contract hire is to say that you are only paying for what you use – the expected diminution in the market value of the vehicle during the period when you are using it – rather than the whole price of the car. In other words, you are paying for the expected depreciation (plus of course interest).

If the agreement includes maintenance the supplier will pay for all standard servicing and maintenance work, a certain number of replacement tyres and the annual tax disc, but won't pay costs arising if the vehicle is damaged, neglected or wilfully mistreated.

The rental in a maintenance-inclusive contract includes the supplier's estimate of the cost of maintaining the vehicle. If the estimate is too low, the supplier will make a loss; if too high, it will make a profit. Through this mechanism it is said that the supplier takes the 'maintenance risk' in the vehicle.

With contract hire you are buying more than just a financial product: you are getting a service so you need to be sure that the supplier can deliver the service that meets your needs.

You can normally choose whatever lease period you require,

though many contract hire companies will refuse to lease you a vehicle for less than 12 months or more than 5 years.

Almost all contract hire rentals stay fixed regardless of changes in market interest rates, unexpected service costs or fluctuations in the used car market.

The lease will set out the maximum vehicle mileage allowed during the lease period. The leasing company will have based their rental calculation on this mileage. Obviously, if the vehicle is only likely to cover a low mileage its true depreciation (the loss of market value) and maintenance costs will be lower than those of a similar vehicle covering more miles, so you will pay a lower rental.

If the agreed contract mileage is exceeded, you will have to pay the *excess mileage charge* specified in the agreement, to compensate the supplier for the additional depreciation and maintenance costs it will incur.

It has become fashionable to call excess mileage charges 'penalties' but this is an unfair expression. These charges should just ensure that you pay for the mileage actually covered by the vehicle, as if the rental had been based on this mileage from the outset.

If you lease several vehicles from one supplier, pooled mileage will normally be included in the agreement. This allows any under-mileage driven by one car to be credited against over-mileage in another, thus reducing the net excess mileage charge.

We've already discussed the corporation tax and VAT rules for leased vehicles, so I won't repeat them here. The written quote you receive from the contract hire company will split the rental between finance and maintenance elements, so you can see the net cost of the car after VAT. The quote will also show the car's CO_2 emissions, so you can see whether you will get full corporation tax relief on the lease rental and your driver can calculate how much car benefit tax they will have to pay on their company car.

Contract hire isn't all about price. You are buying a service and should choose a supplier according to the balance you require between service and price.

Leasing companies are usually happy to allow you to extend a lease at the end of the contract period so long as your payments are not in arrears and the vehicle has not already cost a great deal to maintain. You will be offered either an informal extension (for a few months, usually at the same rental as before) or a formal extension (normally for 6+ months, at a revised rental).

At the end of the lease period the contract hire company will contact you to arrange to collect the vehicle from the address of your choice. On collection the agent will complete a report for both parties to sign, confirming that the vehicle has been handed over and whether there has been any damage to the vehicle.

It is in both parties' interests that this report should be as accurate as possible to avoid later disputes about the condition of the vehicle. Bear in mind that if the car is dirty, the light is poor or the weather is bad it may be difficult for the condition of the vehicle to be assessed accurately.

The contract hire agreement will say that the vehicle has to be returned at the end of the lease in good condition 'fair wear and tear for the age and mileage excepted'. Which leaves us with the question; what is the dividing line between fair wear and tear and unfair damage?

Fortunately, the BVRLA has produced *Fair Wear and Tear Guides* for use by the industry and clients, which carefully define this dividing line.

So, should you use contract hire?

It offers you a comprehensive solution that includes:

- Supply of the vehicle (no need for you to go out and find it).
- Low interest rates built into the rental (often lower than you would get if you searched the market for credit).
- The benefit of big fleet purchasing power.
- Payment of all routine maintenance and servicing bills (no need to scrutinise maintenance bills or negotiate with garages).
- Automatic annual vehicle excise duty renewal.
- An off-balance sheet finance product (though all leases may be 'on balance sheet' soon).
- No residual value risk.
- No maintenance cost risk.

The success of the product has been its simplicity. You get a vehicle for an agreed term and mileage and just hand it back at the end of the lease. So long as the agreed mileage has not been exceeded and the vehicle is undamaged, that's all that needs to happen.

The contract hire market is highly competitive. If you wish you can simply shop around on a car-by-car basis to find the lowest quote and take your cars from a variety of suppliers, though you'll lose out on pooled mileage, have more paperwork and will have to manage a number of supplier relationships.

The main disadvantage of contract hire is that it involves giving away an element of flexibility. You will feel this most acutely if you decide to early terminate the lease or if the mileage you drive exceeds the contract mileage. If you need to be able to change your vehicles at short notice or you are in a high staff-turnover business, you may find that the early termination charges become burdensome. If you own your own vehicles you can do as you wish. For some, this is important.

Whilst early termination charges can be annoying it's worthwhile mentioning that these are largely designed to compensate the leasing company for the loss they suffer when they dispose of the vehicle earlier than planned. If you were to buy the vehicle outright rather than lease it, you would suffer this loss too. You wouldn't receive an invoice for the early termination but would still have to write off the loss as additional depreciation in your books.

Taxation and financial mathematics are a central part of this book so it won't come as a surprise when I advise you to do a full tax-based discounted cash flow analysis before choosing your financial product. Contract hire is the cheapest option for many vehicles for many organisations, but, as we saw in earlier chapters, this isn't always the case.

You should seriously consider using contract hire if the financial analysis shows it is beneficial and you believe that the advantages listed above outweigh the disadvantages for your business.

21

OTHER LEASES

In the previous chapter we looked at contract hire, the most popular form of vehicle finance in the UK by far. In this chapter we will look at open book leasing (a variant of contract hire) and finance leases.

If you have a large fleet, your contract hire company may be willing to give you a share of any profit they make in maintaining or selling your vehicles.

There are several ways these schemes can operate but they all involve the supplier sending you initial information about how your rentals have been calculated, and following this up with reports showing the actual v budgeted maintenance costs and vehicle sale proceeds. We can group all of these schemes together under the heading '**open-book leasing**'.

Suppliers may offer you a proportion of any profit they make on maintaining or selling your vehicles, perhaps 25%. Sometimes the percentages are different; for example, 25% of maintenance profit and 50% of used vehicle sale profit.

Normally open-book leasing is only available if you have at least 10 or 15 vehicles that will come off lease in a given period. This allows the supplier to net off losses on some vehicles against profits on others, so that you only receive the net profit, if any. The calculation period is usually 12 months but for a big fleet it could be 3 or 6 months, to avoid building up big balances.

You might wonder why a leasing company would wish to give away a chunk of its profit whilst retaining any losses. The answer is that it generates a competitive advantage – not all suppliers will do this. It also encourages clients to remain loyal to the supplier. Indeed in most open book deals the client only uses one supplier. Leasing companies prefer to have a long term relationship with a client rather than having to run around trying to win new ones, and they are therefore prepared to give away part of their potential profit in order to sweeten the relationship.

Historically, there has been another reason why leasing companies have offered profit shares to large clients whilst retaining any losses. If the lessee had assumed any of the loss, this would mean that they were bearing some of the risks and rewards of ownership of the vehicles, which would almost definitely have meant that those vehicles would have to be capitalised on the lessee's balance sheet. There are significant changes on the horizon for lease accounting which we won't go into here, save to pose a question: if all leases will one day be on balance sheet, will that mean that leasing companies will start offering a different type of profit share deal to their clients, in which the leasing company and the client share profits *and losses* on residual values and/or maintenance costs? The answer is, quite possibly.

Open-book leasing has several advantages. Lessors offer it because it tends to generate long term relationships. Open-book clients also tend to look after their cars better because they have a vested interest in the return condition of the vehicle. Lessees like these deals because they can be very valuable; delivering cheaper motoring and a good, close, long term relationship with a trusted supplier who comes to understand the client's business and is therefore able to anticipate the client's needs.

However, many lessees are wary of these schemes, believing the money the fleet company paid back to them was their own money in the first place, leaving a feeling that they gave the supplier an interest-free loan for the period of the lease.

Although it's not a product per se, we have to mention **sale and lease back**. This is the name for the transaction where you sell your vehicles to a lessor, then continue to use them under the terms of a leasing agreement, usually contract hire.

There are a variety of reasons why you may wish to do this, for example, to:

■ raise cash

■ remove residual value risk

■ reduce your administration or

■ remove the vehicles from your balance sheet

Or perhaps, having decided to use contract hire for the first time, you decide to sell your existing fleet to the contract hire company so that you can immediately start to enjoy the service advantages rather than waiting up to three years until the whole fleet has been replaced piecemeal.

Sale and lease back is often called 'purchase and lease back' or simply 'leaseback' and many companies have found that it is a valuable step to take when migrating from outright purchase to contract hire.

The next lease product we need to consider is **finance lease**.

A finance lease is defined in Statement of Standard Accounting Practice 21 as a lease that transfers "substantially all of the risks and rewards of ownership of the asset to the lessee".

In plain English this means that it puts the lessee in much the same position as they would have been if they had bought the asset.

A finance lease is a financing device. It gives you an alternative way to obtain the use of a vehicle other than hire purchase, conditional sale or one of the other methods of vehicle purchase. It is also known as a 'full pay-out lease' or, in the United States, an 'open-ended' lease.

The general assumption with a finance lease is that there will be only one lessee. This distinguishes it from contract hire, where the lessor either has to lease the vehicle to several parties in succession or to sell it before they recover their investment.

In a finance lease, the lessor will charge you rentals that are sufficient to fully repay their investment during the primary period of the lease; that is, to clear their books. You are committed to paying the rentals for this period.

A finance lease is therefore said to be non-cancellable. This is rather odd, because almost all leasing companies will early terminate a finance lease as willingly as a contract hire agreement. Nonetheless, finance leases are still considered by many to be non-cancellable.

The key difference between a finance lease and contract hire is the treatment of the vehicle at the end of the lease. Depending on the wording of the finance lease agreement, one (or more) of the following will occur:

■ You will sell the vehicle as the lessor's agent

■ You will allow the lessor to recover the vehicle and sell it or

■ You will elect to enter into a secondary lease period.

Whoever sells the vehicle, the lessor will retain a small proportion of the sale proceeds and you will retain the balance, which is normally given to you as a rebate of rentals.

It is worthwhile dwelling for a moment on how this normally works.

In a finance lease you have an obligation to pay all of the rentals, including the balloon rental. Once you have paid these the lessor will have fully recovered its investment in the vehicle, covered its interest and other costs and made a profit. But it still owns the vehicle and the lease will stipulate very clearly that you cannot become the owner.

To ensure that the lessor does not then sell the vehicle, retain the sales proceeds and make a windfall profit, the lease will stipulate an amount of money they have to pass back to you once the vehicle has been sold. This will normally be paid as a rebate of rentals, which makes it clear that, for tax purposes, the payment is a revenue (trading) item rather than a capital receipt of sales proceeds. Typically, the amount payable might be 95% of the sale proceeds of the vehicle.

Technically, the lessor has to:

- Invoice you for the balloon rental
- Receive this payment from you
- Sell the vehicle
- Receive the sales proceeds
- Raise a credit note to you for 95% of the sales proceeds and then
- Refund this to you.

In reality, many lessors do not collect the balloon payment but simply raise an invoice for this amount and a credit note for the rebate of rentals, then pay you (or ask you to pay) the difference.

A finance lease has two distinct phases. The **primary period** is the initial non-cancellable period of the lease and runs for the fixed period set out in the agreement. By the end of this period the lessor will normally have no balance outstanding in its books for this lease.

This is followed by the **secondary period**, which may last for an indefinite period of time in which the lessor allows you to continue leasing the vehicle. This period ends either when the parties agree or when the vehicle is sold.

Vehicle finance leases often stipulate that a balloon rental is payable at the end of the primary period. The payment is usually the equivalent of the estimated residual value of the vehicle, which means that the monthly amount payable under a finance lease will often be similar to the rentals in a contract hire agreement (excluding maintenance). The difference, of course, is that you are obliged to pay the balloon rental in the finance lease but not in contract hire.

Normally, the secondary period rental will be much less than the primary period rental and may only amount to a few per cent of the capital cost of the vehicle. This is often called a peppercorn rental, reflecting the fact that a peppercorn is an item of very little value. Its primary purpose is to provide your ongoing acknowledgement that the vehicle is still under lease and that you are not the owner. You cannot just sell it and retain the proceeds.

You will normally be responsible for the maintenance of the vehicle, though if required the lessor may add a maintenance package to the agreement (as in contract hire), or they may offer to pay for maintenance and recharge the cost to you as it is incurred.

The VAT treatment of finance leases is the same as for contract hire but the corporation tax treatment can be different. A government order called **SP3/91** says you cannot get accelerated corporation tax relief by paying uneven rentals, e.g. large initial rentals. If uneven rentals are payable you get corporation tax relief on the rentals on a straight-line basis.

As you are bearing the residual value risk on the vehicle, it has to be shown on your balance sheet.

Normally, finance leases are offered as fixed interest rate products. The rentals remain fixed so you have no risk if interest rates change. Some financiers offer variable interest rate finance leases too.

Most vehicle lessees shun finance leases, perceiving that these offer few advantages over contract hire. So finance leasing only represents approximately 1% of the business vehicle finance market.

22

MORE FINANCE PRODUCTS

In the last couple of chapters we've looked at various ways a company can fund its vehicles, including outright purchase, hire purchase, finance lease and contract hire. In this chapter we look at even more funding methods.

Contract hire has been popular for decades but by the early 1980s it was apparent that it did not work for all businesses. Companies that were exempt or partially exempt for VAT purposes couldn't recover some or all of the VAT charged on the lease rentals. Also, many companies didn't use contract hire for their expensive vehicles because at that time there was a permanent corporation tax disallowance on rentals for 'expensive' cars.

The contract hire industry responded by creating a new product – **contract purchase**.

The concept was quite simple: by putting three agreements together a client could be given all of the advantages of contract hire without these VAT or corporation tax disadvantages.

Those three agreements were:

■ A conditional sale or hire purchase agreement containing a lump-sum ('balloon') payment at the end of the contract

■ A repurchase undertaking

■ A maintenance agreement

Under the conditional sale or hire purchase agreement the client agreed to buy the vehicle on deferred purchase terms (by paying instalments over a period of time).

The repurchase undertaking said that the contract hire company would, at the client's option, buy the vehicle back at the end of the contract for a pre-agreed fixed price.

The maintenance agreement covered the standard maintenance items normally found in a maintenance-inclusive contract hire agreement.

As the finance agreement was a purchase-type agreement, no VAT was chargeable on the payments and the permanent tax disallowance on lease rentals did not apply. The maintenance agreement was separate so it was clear that the client could recover VAT on the maintenance payments.

It is fair to say that this arrangement attracted the early attention of HM Revenue and Customs because it denied Customs the VAT it might otherwise have expected to receive. There were a number of well-publicised cases where contract hire companies had to withdraw contract purchase agreements that were challenged by Customs and to reissue them after consultation with legal counsel.

In 1995 there was a change in the VAT rules and leasing companies were allowed to recover VAT when buying vehicles to lease to clients. Most other businesses remained unable to recover this input VAT. This change in the law led to a general reduction in contract hire rentals. This tilted the lease v buy equation in favour of leasing and contract hire, thus adding another variable into the analysis that fleet managers had to carry out when deciding which financial product to use to acquire their vehicles.

The uncertainties of the early years of contract purchase are now long gone and it now a common form of vehicle finance. Most lessors now combine the three agreements – conditional sale (or hire purchase), maintenance and buy-back – into one document.

Contract purchase is widely used by companies and is also the basis of a very popular method of consumer motor finance called **personal contract purchase**.

Contract purchase is similar to contract hire but there are important differences. As the contract purchase contract is legally a conditional sale or hire purchase agreement under which you are buying the vehicle, it is an 'on balance sheet' product.

The pre-agreed repurchase price that the supplier agrees to pay represents their estimate of the likely future value of the vehicle. This is called the guaranteed repurchase price, the guaranteed minimum purchase value or the guaranteed minimum future value (GMFV). The supplier takes the risk of whether you will sell the vehicle back to them and the market price of the vehicle if you do so.

Contract purchase represents less than 5% of the fleet finance market, reflecting the fact that it is a niche product.

Contract purchase gives you the option to buy or return the vehicle, as well as the tax advantages described above. It offers predictable costs and you only pay VAT on the maintenance element. As with outright purchase, contract purchase is currently an 'on balance sheet' form of finance.

You might also use contract purchase if you like the idea of having an option to either buy the vehicle or hand it back to the supplier at the end of the contract.

Many companies use **loans** to finance their vehicles. These are usually unsecured: that is, the lender cannot repossess and sell the vehicle if the borrower stops paying. So unless your business has high financial strength, the interest rate will be high to compensate for the fact that the lender lacks security.

An exception to this is where the lender holds a debenture or charge – a registered security that gives them fixed and floating charges over specific assets owned by the borrower.

A charge is a mortgage over property, a right you give a lender/lessor to deal with your assets in the event of your default. It is registered at Companies House and on your company's register of charges. Charges give the lender security (i.e. rights) in your assets. The lender can take possession of those assets, control them and sell them if you fail to meet your obligations.

Charges can be fixed, in which case they list the specific assets to which they relate, for instance, the vehicles in your fleet. Or they can be floating, in which case they give the lender security over a general class of assets over which you have title, the nature of which changes over time (for example, debtors).

If the lender has a fixed charge over an asset, any sale of the asset may be ineffective, and even if it is effective the buyer buys the asset subject to the charge.

A floating charge becomes fixed when the borrower or hirer defaults on their obligations.

There are lots of advantages to using loans. They are very widely available, can be obtained at fixed or variable interest rates and for short or long periods. You can use them to fund one asset or many. They are simple to administer and require no knowledge of lease accounting. Variable rate loans can usually be repaid without penalty. Loan interest is normally deductible as a business expense for corporation (or income) tax purposes. Having used the loan to buy your vehicles you can claim capital allowances.

The downsides are that vehicles financed on loans have to be capitalised on your balance sheet and – importantly – when most companies borrow money to buy a car they are unable to recover any input VAT tax on the purchase price.

Bank overdrafts are the most widely used form of business finance in the UK. Most companies, including most cash-rich ones, have an overdraft facility.

The operation of an overdraft could not be simpler. You agree an overdraft limit with your bank manager and then you deposit funds and draw cheques in the normal course of your business. Once every month or quarter you are charged interest on the amount of the overdraft that you have used, for the number of days you have used it.

An overdraft is normally secured by a debenture. It is always provided as a variable rate interest product, the interest rate being quoted as a margin over the base rate of the bank that supplies it.

Bank overdrafts are cheap to set up and, as you only pay for what you use, they are cheap to use.

Many companies use overdrafts to fund their vehicles but it is probably not best practice to do so. Overdrafts are a type of **working capital**. That is, they provide you with cash to finance the trade cycle; the time lag between buying goods and services to make your product and being paid by your customer. If you use your overdraft to finance long term assets, such as vehicles, you will drain your company of its working capital.

Conventional business thinking is that you should use short term money (loans, other short term borrowings, overdrafts) to finance the trade cycle and other short-held assets. You should use longer term borrowings (leases, hire purchase, long term loans) to finance the acquisition of longer term assets (vehicles, plant and equipment, etc.). Very long term assets, such as property, should be financed on very long term borrowings, such as mortgages or by issuing share capital.

It is a truism, but companies don't collapse because they make losses. They collapse because they don't have the money to pay the wages at the end of the month. If you borrow money for the correct period, your company will not risk becoming starved for cash in the short term simply through having used up its short term funds to buy long term assets.

Most overdrafts are offered as variable rate products. If you finance your vehicles on overdraft for three years you will be exposed to interest rate changes during that time. If rates rise, the actual cost of financing the vehicle may end up being much more than you had planned.

If your company is **cash rich** – i.e. you have strong cash balances in the bank and have no need to borrow – you may never have considered leasing because you see it as a form of borrowing.

However, leasing can be attractive to cash-rich businesses. It allows them to lease vehicles at a capital cost based on a pre-VAT price, because, unlike most other businesses, leasing companies can recover the input VAT when buying vehicles. This is not possible for most UK businesses.

Leasing also takes away the residual value risk.

Do bear in mind that whatever financial product you use, you can always use fleet management products (purchasing, maintenance control, disposal, administration, etc.) to outsource non-core activities and get the benefit of fleet discounts, expertise and risk management.

23

EMPLOYEE CAR OWNERSHIP AND SALARY SACRIFICE SCHEMES

IN THIS CHAPTER...

- The two newest fleet funding products

- The tax basis for these products

- Calculating the tax impacts

- Cash allowances

- Risks and benefits

In this chapter we will wrap up the fleet funding topic with a look at the two newest fleet funding products:

- employee car ownership schemes and

- salary sacrifice schemes

These schemes make clever use of the tax system and can deliver real savings to employers and employees. They show the fleet leasing industry at its best: recognising the need for new products to work in specific circumstances and then inventing the solution.

Employee car ownership schemes were first developed in the early 1990s in response to the relatively high levels of company car tax.

Someone noticed that Section 157 Income and Corporation Taxes Act 1988 says:

(1)   Where … in the case of a person employed in director's or higher-paid employment, a car is made available (without any transfer of the property in it) either to himself or to others being members of his family or household, and—

    a)   it is so made available by reason of his employment and it is in that year available for his or their private use; and

    b)   the benefit of the car is not (apart from this section) chargeable to tax as the employee's income,

    there is to be treated as emoluments of the employment, and accordingly chargeable to income tax under Schedule E, an amount equal to whatever is the cash equivalent of that benefit in that year.

In plain English this means that if a car is made available to a director or higher-paid employee by reason of their employment they should pay income tax on the car benefit.

Now look again at the words in brackets "without any transfer of the property in it". These words mean that if there is a transfer of title in the car the employee is not subject to car benefit tax.

So if a scheme can be put together where title *does* pass to the employee, it will be outside the scope of car benefit tax. This does not mean that it will avoid taxation completely, just the company car benefit tax.

This is the legal provision that allowed ECO schemes to be established.

On the surface these schemes look like conventional contract hire; a leasing company provides the car and all the various services. However the schemes use credit sale agreements as the underlying financial product, rather than leases or conditional sale agreements. Under a credit sale agreement title in the vehicle passes immediately to the employee at the inception of the agreement, so no car benefit tax is payable.

There are many hurdles to trip the unwary, however, and parts of any such scheme may cause other taxable benefits to arise.

These schemes are complex, can be expensive to set up and require ongoing management and tax consultancy.

The employer gives the employee a cash allowance which needs to be amended if there is a change in:

■ the driver's circumstances (e.g. their business or personal mileage),

■ the rate of income tax they pay

■ general rates of corporation tax or

■ National Insurance contribution rates.

These schemes are generally unsuited to companies with high levels of staff turnover.

HM Revenue and Customs has been willing to check and pre-approve ECO schemes – a sensible precaution for any employer or supplier.

These schemes are not 'tax evasion' and are perfectly acceptable to HMRC. They have even issued detailed instructions to tax inspectors on how to review these schemes and a lengthy HMRC review concluded that no additional tax needs to be levied on properly-constituted ECO schemes.

There is a parallel to be drawn between an employee car ownership scheme and a final salary pension scheme. The employer takes on an open-ended risk on both.

ECOS represents perhaps 3% of the fleet market.

If correctly established, an employee car ownership scheme will allow an employee to have all of the advantages of a company car, while their employer, and possibly also the employee, will save money.

The disadvantages are that these schemes are extremely costly to set up, can require long term assistance and consultancy from external experts and require reworking every time there is a change in tax rates or rules.

If you are keen to explore these schemes, the message is the same as with any other major change: shop around, do your research, involve all interested parties within your business (e.g. purchasing, human resources, finance, legal) and only proceed when you are sure that it will not cause major problems to your business.

We now need to consider another product, **salary sacrifice**.

Let's consider what happens when a company leases its cars from a contract hire company. The supplier almost definitely buy cars and other services for less than the client would pay. Almost all leased cars are supplied new, and replaced every few years, so they are modern and fuel-efficient. The income tax system encourages drivers to choose low-CO_2 cars to save tax. The supplier administers all of the servicing and repairs, and supplies the annual tax disk.

This is an efficient, low cost and environmentally-friendly way for any company to obtain its cars.

Now let's consider an employee who doesn't have a company car but uses their own car for work and claims a mileage allowance for business mileage. Who ensures that this car is regularly serviced and the MOT is up to date? Their employer has a statutory duty to ensure the car is safe but who checks to ensure it is insured for business purposes and is safe to be on the road?

The average UK car is 6.7 years old, and there's no particular reason to think that employees' own cars are any younger. Therefore these cars are generally less reliable, more likely to have breakdowns and have higher CO_2 emissions than leased cars.

Neither of these employees would be able to do their jobs without their cars. But clearly the lease car arrangement is superior for a whole range of reasons.

Salary Sacrifice is a solution to these issues. Salary sacrifice schemes use tax benefits to encourage employees to stop driving their own cars for business mileage and to use leased vehicles instead. The employee agrees to forego part of their salary and their company gives them another benefit instead – the use of a leased company car.

The company saves the sacrificed salary and Class 1 national insurance (NIC), and then pays for the car lease and the Class 1A NIC. The employee pays benefit in kind tax but this will be low if they choose a car with a relatively low level of CO_2. Taken together, significant amounts of tax and NIC can be saved, though the tax saving is just one of the many advantages of salary sacrifice.

A properly set up salary sacrifice scheme can deliver a number of benefits for a company:

- Income tax savings for their employees
- National insurance savings for both the employee and company
- A valuable recruitment and retention tool
- A reduction in their risks under health and safety and corporate manslaughter legislation.
- CO_2 emissions reductions
- Less chance the employee will call in to say their car won't start
- Assurance that employees are insured to drive for work
- An end to the practice whereby the employer pays more than necessary for work-related mileage
- Delivery of a valuable new employment benefit at no additional cost to the employer. Indeed, the employer can expect to save money

There are a number of steps you need to go through to set up a salary sacrifice scheme, including changing contracts of employment, modifying payroll systems, communicating with employees, promoting the scheme and so on.

Whilst salary sacrifice is novel for the company car market, these schemes have been around for years for other types of benefit such as childcare vouchers and free health screening. They generate real savings if the employee pays less income tax on the benefit than on the salary, e.g. when they choose a low-emission car.

The lease for salary sacrifice vehicles will typically include all of the features the employer would normally specify on their normal company car leases, e.g. servicing, maintenance, replacement tyres, UK emergency roadside recovery, accident management, annual road tax renewal, etc. Some schemes also include an annual drivers' licence check.

Once the car has been delivered the employer deducts a monthly amount from the employee's gross salary to cover the cost of providing the vehicle. The employee sacrifices as much salary they wish so long as this does not make their gross salary less than the national minimum wage.

If you are thinking of setting up a salary sacrifice scheme you should be prepared to commit some time and effort to getting it set up and launched, though your leasing company will help with some aspects of this.

There are many aspects to consider.

If the employee takes maternity, paternity, adoption or sick leave, the employer must legally continue to provide all employment benefits, including the salary sacrifice car.

Future salary increases and pension contributions will need to be based on the employee's pre-sacrifice salary (the 'notional salary'), rather than the new gross salary, so you will have to keep a record of employees' notional salaries, which may require a change to your HR and payroll systems.

You will also need to decide how to deal with minor vehicle damage such as 'kerbed' wheels and minor bodywork damage that isn't covered by insurance. Will you recharge the cost to the employee or will your company bear the cost?

You also need rules governing what happens when an employee leaves your company. The leasing company may wish to terminate the lease. Who will pay the early termination charges?

There are a number of risks:

- You invest time and effort in setting up the scheme and take-up is low

- The scheme is incorrectly set up so does not generate the expected tax and NIC benefits

- Future changes in income tax or NIC legislation, or HMRC practice, that adversely affect the economics of these schemes

- Early termination charges

- Damage recharge costs

- You don't handle the payroll issues correctly, e.g. the salary sacrifice, SSP, SMP, notional salary, paternity leave, etc.

Many of these risks can be mitigated by setting up the scheme properly. Do bear in mind that whilst current legislation allows salary sacrifice schemes to flourish, and there is no sign this is likely to change, no-one can be sure that this will not change at some time in the future.

24

CASH-FOR-CAR: INTRODUCTION

IN THIS CHAPTER...

- When the employer simply provides the employee with more salary

- Different approaches

- Allocating the savings

- Approved Mileage Allowance Payments (AMAPs)

- Class 1 and Class 1A National Insurance

We have now considered all of the major forms of vehicle finance, including employee car ownership schemes (ECOS) and salary sacrifice schemes.

In this chapter we are going to step back and look more broadly at the issues that arise when an employer stops providing a company car and simply provides the employee with more salary instead.

The company car tax system clearly works to the disadvantage of many company car drivers. For some, the company car no longer represents good value because the tax they pay exceeds the cost they would incur if they simply took extra salary from their employer and acquired their own car.

Some employers – particularly those with lots of 'perk' cars – have long believed that the administration of a car fleet is an unnecessary burden. In the mid-1990s, American businesses operating in the UK started to move away from company cars and simply added an amount to their employees' salaries to compensate for the withdrawal of the car. The perk car culture is less well established in the USA and these companies had always questioned whether they should be providing company cars.

Rising levels of car benefit tax gave them and other employers the opportunity to withdraw this benefit and to replace it with cash payments: *cash-for-car*.

If their company car is withdrawn, many employees still need a car in order to carry out their jobs. Employers have adopted several different approaches:

■ Some have allowed their staff to choose between taking a company car and receiving extra salary. Employees like to have a cash option available to them, even when they don't take it up.

■ Some have introduced employer-sponsored personal contract purchase schemes (PCP), in which they introduce their staff to a leasing company that provides fully maintained cars.

- Some have introduced employee car ownership schemes (ECOs), which change the legal structure of the company car scheme but leave the operational aspects largely unchanged (see earlier chapter)

- Some have introduced salary sacrifice schemes (see last chapter)

- And some have stopped providing cars altogether, paid extra salary and left their employees to fend for themselves.

Cash-for-car schemes can generate significant savings. As an employer you will need to decide who will benefit from these.

If the company keeps all of the savings you may find it hard to encourage employees to opt out of their company cars.

If the savings are shared between the company and the employees you have to decide how these will be split.

If the savings are all passed to the employees you will encourage take-up but this is not ideal for the shareholders.

If you decide to introduce a cash-for-car scheme it makes sense to work with a leasing company to help your employees get a car through a lease or PCP agreement.

Given the choice between cash or car, an employee has to decide which to take. They have to calculate their cash receipts and payments (including tax) under both scenarios, and a good employer will help them to do this. These calculations are complicated. Doing the sums and explaining them to a single driver is time-consuming but for a large group it is a major exercise though here again a leasing company could help you.

There is a danger that a badly set up cash-for-car scheme will fail to remove the car benefit tax from the employee. You should be wary of guaranteeing your employees' payment obligations (or actually paying these liabilities) under PCP or PCH arrangements. You may trigger a tax liability.

In all cases, it makes sense to talk to HM Revenue and Customs.

If you provide a cash allowance in lieu of a company car you will save the cost of the Class 1A National Insurance contributions. Any cash allowance you pay to an employee in lieu of his company car will be fully taxable. You will pay Class 1 employer's NIC and the employee will pay Class 1 NIC on the cash allowance.

You will need to pay a mileage allowance when the employee uses their private vehicle on company business. So long as this is not above the level of HM Revenue and Customs Approved Mileage Allowance Payments (AMAP) the employee will have no tax or NIC liability on these payments. If the mileage rate paid is less than the AMAP, the employee can claim the shortfall as an additional amount of tax relief in their tax return.

If the payment exceeds the AMAP levels, the excess over the AMAP level will be taxable at the employee's marginal rate.

If you decide to adopt a cash-for-car scheme it makes sense to pay the employee the full amount of the AMAP (on which they pay no tax or National Insurance contributions) and a lower level of cash allowance (on which they pay tax and possibly Class 1 National Insurance, and on which the employer pays Class 1A National Insurance).

This could be better than paying a higher cash allowance and a lower mileage rate.

You can give employees interest-free loans of up to £5,000 to help them buy their own vehicles. There is no income tax charge on this benefit so long as the loan is fully repayable, and it is indeed repaid and not written-off. This loan can be used as a deposit towards a finance scheme or lease agreement and it will therefore reduce the monthly payments the employee has to make to the funder/lessor. In practice, most employers prefer not to offer such a loan.

You need to give very careful consideration to setting up a cash-for-car scheme and also decide whether any savings should be kept by the company or shared with the employees.

With cash-for-car there are a number of operational and HR issues to consider, and we will cover these next.

25

CASH-FOR-CAR: OPERATIONAL AND HR ISSUES

IN THIS CHAPTER...

- Decisions you will need to make

- Motor insurance issues

- Vehicle selection and allocation

- Consumer credit licence

- Staff motivation

Having looked at some of the tax and structural issues to consider with cash-for-car: schemes, we now need to consider some operational and HR issues.

We'll start by looking at **operational issues**.

Selecting, test-driving, buying, maintaining, insuring and disposing of a car all involve an element of hassle. With company cars the employer has the hassle. With many cash-for-car arrangements it is left with the employees, who will most likely do these tasks during working hours when they should be concentrating on their day-jobs.

When implementing a cash-for-car scheme you will have to make some important policy decisions.

In many company car schemes, employees are allowed to select a car from a list, according to their staff grade. When introducing cash-for-car schemes, many employers try to replace these car bands with cash bands; "If you are at such-and-such a grade you are entitled to receive £400 per month instead of a company car".

However, if two employees are earning the same salary and doing the same job but don't drive the same business mileage, paying them identical cash and mileage allowances will leave one substantially better off than the other. They will be unable to afford the same car.

Generally these schemes work best when employees have a good idea of the level of business mileage they will drive – but many don't.

What happens if a driver moves job inside the organisation and now drives more or fewer miles than planned? Who pays the additional costs or gets the savings, the employer or the employee?

Motor insurance can be problematic. Employees don't build up no-claims bonuses while driving the company's vehicles.

Therefore, some employees who have opted for cash allowances have discovered that motor insurers have quoted very large premiums and have not recognised their years of accident- and claim-free motoring. The better cash-for-car schemes recognise this issue and include arrangements with the companies' insurers to continue to cover those members of staff who opt for cash. After all, the insurers still want the business and the risk has not changed.

Vehicle selection can be an issue. Where cars are used in your business (for example, by salespeople) you might think it reasonable for the company to stipulate the type, age and quality of car that can be used on company business. But the employee can reasonably say they should be able to spend their income on whatever they want. In practice, many cash-for-car schemes limit the cars that employees can use on company business, e.g. no sports cars, nothing over four years old and no two-door cars.

Where schemes are less prescriptive than this, many employees now enjoy the newly-found freedom to choose whatever car they want, and many have selected quality used vehicles to stretch their cash allowance further.

Some schemes allow the employer to deduct cash from salary and pay this directly to a leasing company. Lessors prefer this as it reduces their administration and gives them one point of contact.

If employees use their own cars on company business, the cars must comply with health and safety legislation and be properly serviced, maintained and insured (for business). These cars should be included in your health and safety assessments.

You may need a consumer credit licence from the Office of Fair Trading if you plan to help your employees organise car finance. It is hard to get the OFT to be prescriptive about who does and doesn't need a licence. However, it seems that if you simply advertise a leasing company's PCP scheme on your intranet and invite staff to apply direct to the leasing company, you will not require a licence. But if you administer the finance application process, handle the application forms, arrange for the agreements to be signed, etc., you will be doing the same job as a broker and your business has to be licensed.

Turning now to **human resource** issues, there has been much debate on how employees can be encouraged to take up cash-for-car schemes.

Some consultants insist that all employees can be pushed into them on the same day without any problems.

However, if your company's standard employment contract says you will provide employees with a car, you cannot unilaterally withdraw this benefit. If the contract allows you to withdraw or modify this benefit at your sole discretion, you are free to make whatever changes you wish, though you may well have a very unhappy workforce if you impose a scheme on them.

Employees are rarely enthusiastic when facing withdrawal of their company cars. Once their cars are gone, many will have to enter into finance agreements to obtain their cars, committing to pay thousands of pounds over a number of years. If they have concerns about job security (for example, if the company has made people redundant recently, or if they have received adverse comments about their personal performance) they will be reluctant to make this commitment. If they are planning to move home they may have concerns about their ability to raise a mortgage and having to disclose several thousand pounds of additional indebtedness to potential lenders.

In some cash-for-car schemes the employer organises accident, sickness and redundancy insurance for the employees through an insurance company. It may seem strange for the employer to organise redundancy cover but it provides an important safety cushion for their employees.

Salary is normally the starting point for calculating some employee benefits; particularly pension contributions. As a cash-for-car scheme involves adding a sum of money to the employees' salaries, most schemes specifically state that the cash allowance shall be excluded when calculating pension benefits.

So, you should you introduce a cash-for-car scheme?

Introduced correctly, they can be motivational. They can allow the individual employee the freedom to choose their own vehicle, save money for the employer and save lot of administration.

Introduced incorrectly they can expose your drivers to financial risks, have a demotivating effect and expose your company to new health and safety risks.

26

ROUNDING OFF

If you've made your way step-by-step through this book you've covered a lot of ground.

You should now be able to calculate the answer to the question, "Should I should lease or buy my vehicles?"

You know how to use discounted cash flow analysis to do these calculations and you are familiar with concepts such as the time value of money and discount factors. The standard discounting formula

$$PV = \sum_{1}^{36} \frac{PMT^n}{(1 + i)^n}$$

holds no fear for you.

Along the way you have picked up some useful Excel skills. By now you should know how to use Excel to calculate the monthly finance instalment (or rental) if you know the interest rate, and how to calculate the interest rate if you know the monthly instalment.

You know the difference between various types of interest rate: simple, flat rate, compound, nominal, true and APR.

You're an absolute whizz at using Excel to do a complex DCF calculations and love using Goal Seek.

You enjoy using Excel PMT function to calculate lease rentals, the PV function to calculate a present value and the RATE function to calculate interest rates.

And know how to bring tax into your lease v buy decision.

Along the way we have looked at some methods for calculating the early termination settlements for leases (percentage of future rentals, actual cost method and sliding scale according to the timing of the early termination) and other finance agreements (the annuity and 'sum of the digits' methods).

We've taken a brief look at different payment profiles – regular initial rental, high initial rental, spread rental and all in advance – then looked at the effect that a residual value or balloon rental will have on rental calculations.

We also looked at fixed and variable rate transactions, FHBR, LIBOR and A & B factors.

We then considered various 'Purchase-type' finance agreements (outright purchase, hire purchase, conditional sale and credit sale).

Then we moved on to look at leases more broadly before we considered all of the different types of product you are likely to come across (contract hire, 'open-book', sale and lease back, finance lease, contract purchase, loans, bank overdrafts, ECO schemes and salary sacrifice schemes).

We rounded off with a look at the features and benefits of cash-for-car schemes.

I hope you have enjoyed reading this book. The financial side of asset finance is not that complicated: it just needs to be approached one step at a time.

If you would like to provide feedback or comment on the book, or if you would like to see some other subject included in any second edition of the book, please contact me at www.tourick.com.

Colin Tourick

BY THE SAME AUTHOR

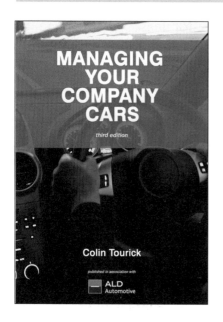

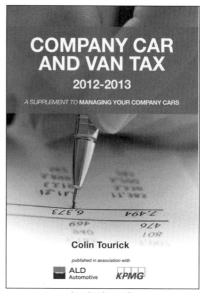

* updated annually

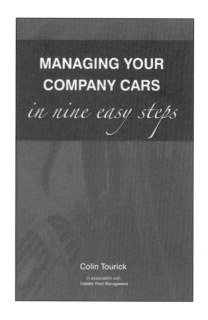

Full details of all titles at www.tourick.com